Principles
of Management
for Quality Projects

■ SMART STRATEGIES SERIES ■

Principles of Management for Quality Projects

Michael C. Carruthers

INTERNATIONAL THOMSON BUSINESS PRESS
I(T)P® An International Thomson Publishing Company

London ● Bonn ● Johannesburg ● Madrid ● Melbourne ● Mexico City ● New York ● Paris
Singapore ● Tokyo ● Toronto ● Albany, NY ● Belmont, CA ● Cincinnati, OH ● Detroit, MI

Principles of Management for Quality Projects

Copyright © 1999 Michael C. Carruthers

I**(T)**P® A division of International Thomson Publishing Inc.
The ITP logo is a trademark under licence

British Library Cataloguing-in-Publication Data
A catalogue record for this book is available from the British Library

This edition published 1999 by International Thomson Business Press

Typeset by LaserScript, Mitcham, Surrey
Printed in the UK by TJ International, Padstow, Cornwall

ISBN 1–86152–522–2

International Thomson Business Press
Berkshire House
168–173 High Holborn
London WC1V 7AA
UK

http://www.itbp.com

Contents

Preface

Projects are a series of activities that are initiated (and completed) to bring about change and a desired end result. The sequence of events that happen during a project usually follow the same or essentially similar patterns, and it is convenient to group these events into various phases of activities.

This document uses three very basic groupings of activities with the following logical activity breakdown for each group. These groupings are as follows:

The pre-project phase, which in turn has three basic sub-groupings:

- Basic assessment

- Pre-feasibility study

- Feasibility study

The project execution phase, which has the following sub-groupings:

- Engineering design and technical

- Procurement of supplies

- Construction and erection

- Precommissioning and handover

- Commissioning

- Contract and project close-out

The operation phase, which has the following sub-groupings:

- Plant (or system) start up

- De-bottlenecking and trouble-shooting, operation and optimization

- Decommissioning

Karl M Wiig, in his chapter on 'Planning for uncertainty in large projects' in *New Dimensions of Project Management*, states that many uncertainties regarding cost and schedule and their implications (and flowing from this the opportunity for error) exist when dealing with the planning of a project. This planning activity which flows from (and often influences) the grouping of activities takes the following into account, i.e:

- the strategies available;

- the characterization of uncertainties and opportunity for errors;

- the implications of implementing the strategy.

It is important to realise that robust, i.e. variation tolerant strategies, must be formulated and met. The strategy options available must be considered very carefully. The project requirements and deliverables must also be quantified. Uncertainties and opportunities for error must be determined, and the implications of undertaking specific strategic options must also be quantified. The parallels between his approach and the one proposed here are clear and, therefore, support the approach.

Each activity within the three basic groupings becomes a task in its own right and a task force is assembled to specifically address the task as a mini-project. This is an adaptation of the task force concept as established by J Robert Fluor, Chairman of the Fluor corporation, in his keynote address to the Project Management Institute, Chicago (1977).

The project manager must be a facilitator to integrate the various disciplines and technologies required. The dedication must be to the project rather than the discipline or function.

The necessity for total integrated planning means that the opportunity for errors due to an oversight decreases considerably. This requires very careful and complete formal formulation of task deliverables and milestones, and out of these detailed requirements, specifications and resultant task definition. These will also form the basis of performance and progress measurement which form the basis of the measurement of quality.

The establishment of the resources required and the resultant planning and scheduling will also follow on from the abovementioned. The correct qualification and quantification of these forms the basis of a successful project (project quality) and a satisfied customer.

This style and approach is similar to the approach proposed by Dr Harold Kerzner in his book *Project Management: A Systems Approach*, when he discusses the life-cycle phases of systems as a progression of the summary of Franklin Moore.

Acknowledgements

The author would like to express his gratitude to all the people with whom he has had the pleasure of working, over many contracts, for their practical mentorship over the past 25 years. He would also like to express his gratitude to his colleagues for their support, reviews critique, ideas and inputs, without which the book in its present form would not have been possible.

Dr H L Roberts, as well as Messrs H J M Paquay, M Boyes, D Johnson, Dr Raymond Loubsher and Leon Snyders are all thanked for their time, support and ideas.

To my wife Elaine, thank you for your assistance with typing, layout and critique which contributed greatly to making the manuscript more user friendly. And especially for her moral support, particularly during the many hours of preparation which limited our time together.

I am grateful for the review and critique of Professor Hans van Vuuren, whose comments, with his many years of project management experience, were especially valuable.

Thank you Connie Luyt, an author in her own right, for her linguistic review, as well as Kay Steyn and Dorothy Labuschagne for the linguistic assistance, review and advice.

The author, who has had the privilege of studying quality directly under such great names as Dr W Edwards Deming, Dr Juran, Professor Gryna and Frank Caplan, has, by virtue of the influence these scholars have had on him, made use of the universal principles that they expound on quality in this book. He wishes to acknowledge the use of their principles and indirect contribution even though they appear in a 'project customized' form.

PART ONE

Introduction

CHAPTER ONE

Introduction: from genesis to fruition

Motivation for this book

A project can be defined as: a series of activities to effect change in a planned and controlled manner to achieve a specific result, that has fixed resources and definite commencement and conclusion dates.

Quality in projects can be defined as the ability to meet the requirements set for the deliverables that have been identified and mutually agreed upon by the customer and the contractor. Such deliverables will satisfy the needs of the customer and the stakeholder(s).

A review by a team of six professionals (who, collectively, have almost 100 years of project management and execution experience) has revealed that only a few of the projects known to them either as case studies or because of personal involvement actually achieved their original purpose, i.e. the complete satisfaction of the customer within the given time limit and within budget (quality).

It was further found that a number of common errors had occurred which, with correct management, could have been avoided. It also transpired that the root cause of approximately 80 per cent of the 'quality problems' experienced was to be found in the management of the project. This conclusion concurs with the findings of Deming (1982) in respect of quality in general, and in the manufacturing and service industries in particular, (i.e. 80 per cent of the problems experienced with quality are caused by poor management).

Many of the problems with quality were symptoms of managerial errors or omissions that could be traced back to the earliest phases of a project. Because of the stringent time and cost limitations that are placed on them, projects are usually event, time and cost driven, with quality (conforming to the long-term requirements of the customer) running a sad fourth.

Very often projects that have been successfully completed within nominal scope, time and cost from the project manager's point of view turn out to be failures in the long term because of operational, product quality and/or marketing problems. The positive or negative influence of quality lasts long after 'cost success' or 'schedule compliance' have been discounted or even forgotten.

CASE STUDY: TOWER BRIDGE

The statistics in respect of London's Tower Bridge, taken from *Mechanical Engineering*, 1995 provide an interesting example of this.

The original estimated cost of the bridge was £585 000 and the time schedule was four years. Construction started in April 1886. The bridge was finally opened on 30 June 1894, eight years after construction had begun. The ultimate cost was £1 million. By modern project standards, this project would have been classified as a failure, with a 100 per cent time overrun and a 70.9 per cent cost overrun. These facts have long faded into history, but the quality aspects of the bridge are manifest even today, a full century later.

The bridge was designed to allow tens of thousands of pedestrians and up to 20 000 horse-drawn vehicles a day to cross the river. Today 10 000 commercial vehicles, some of them weighing 30 tons, cross the bridge every day.

Tower Bridge has never failed to operate during its 100 years' existence, which is a tribute to the quality of its design and manufacture. It has successfully withstood the destructive forces of water pollution and World War II, and is also a major tourist attraction. This is truly an instance where the influence of quality has far outweighed those of cost and schedule. The value that has been added to London, in terms of the international tourism, and as an engineering achievement, has far outweighed the original cost of the project.

It has also been found that as far as projects are concerned, areas where requirements and deliverables are not defined and agreed upon are open to personal interpretation This usually leads to 'extremes', i.e. either 'gold plating' or gross inadequacy, both of which can have serious cost and schedule implications and reflect badly on the ultimate quality of the project.

It is also important to identify the potentially high problem and 'risk-of-error' areas in a project, so that special precautions can be taken to avoid or minimize the risks. It is important to plan and monitor progress in reaching the agreed quality of achieved milestones and to be able to take corrective action where necessary.

Three major phases can usually be identified in project activities. They are the pre-project phase, the project execution phase and the operational phase. There are also many different parties (or players) involved in bringing a project to fruition. Some of these people are pro-actively involved, some re-actively and some even passively. The sum of all the endeavours of the involved parties, during all the different phases and activities, should add up to a successful project when a holistic view is taken.

A holistic approach to managing for quality in projects

One of the most important new developments in the standards required of management against which customer and stakeholder satisfaction is measured can be summed up in the question: 'How successful will the project be as a whole, including the long term?' Management therefore finds itself being measured on many fronts. No matter how well the internal aspects of the project are managed, the ultimate success of the project as a whole relies heavily on the satisfaction of not only the immediate customers – even though they are a very important factor – but also on the satisfaction of the intermittent customers and the affected stakeholders.

Holistic management must therefore look not only at the three traditional measures of project success, that is 'completed within budget', 'on time' and 'of acceptable technical quality', but must go beyond these and also quantify the related aspects in terms of environmental impact. That is, how are the stakeholders, be they human, any other form of life or even landscape beauty, going to be influenced by the advent of the project?

In this regard, the project management team must first concentrate on doing the right things in terms of the project, its objectives and its scope. This means not only the immediate scope of the project, but also the potential related scope and objectives as they affect the environment. Only once these have been fully established and quantified in terms of needs, deliverables and requirements can a full set of project requirements and the real total project scope be formulated. As soon as this has been completed in a satisfactory manner, the other inputs which are better known to project management can be established in order to 'do things right'. Therefore, the philosophy of doing the right things should precede the actions of doing things right, thus achieving both efficiency and effectiveness.

In the past many project organizations and even project customers saw their own personal, immediate goal or the project's immediate goal and scope as the whole. They spent most of their effort in doing things right instead of beginning by spending up to 15 per cent of the project's intellectual effort on establishing the right things to do. This has the effect that the project manager, his customer and potential stakeholders have to work together very closely to ensure a usable, successful project result at the end of the day. A financially unviable project (from a customer's point of view) or an environmentally unacceptable project (from a stakeholder's point of view) is also perceived as a bad reflection on the project management team.

The last major issue that has an impact on the holistic approach is the value of the project to society. Project management should establish what a project's impact will be, both during the project establishment phase, and in terms of the final facility, service or system upon the society that will be affected by the project. A project which society rejects (and there are quite a number of these) will always have a negative influence on the ultimate result. A society that is grossly dissatisfied with the end result of a project because it is either aesthetically unacceptable, noisy, smelly, toxic, unprofitable or environmentally unfriendly can easily have such a facility closed down, either through direct protesting or by means of political lobbying.

The purpose of this work

This book aims to provide the project management professional with a comprehensive guide to the management activities that affect the quality (i.e. conforming to mutually agreed requirements of the deliverables in order to satisfy specific needs) of projects, both directly and indirectly.

The guide is divided into four parts:

- Part 1: An Introduction to the subject; a definition of quality and a description of what it means in the context of a project; the 'people factors' affecting quality in the case of projects.

- Part 2: An insight into the relationship between quality and design, and planning cost.

- Part 3: An outline of some useful quality tools for use by project management.

- Part 4: A matrix and supporting network of generic requirements and deliverables that must be established and complied with by the various parties involved in the various activity stages of a project in order to achieve success as far as quality is concerned.

It is intended to assist the parties involved in the project with the establishment of their input requirements and output deliverables. This will enable them to perform their tasks efficiently, because they will obtain high-quality output from either the previously involved party or the previous activity (as identified in the matrix). This output now becomes part of the input to their specific task.

The requirements and deliverables referred to here are generic and not project-specific. They are, however, intended to cover the philosophical spectrum, and serve as a memory jogger. The requirements and deliverables will have to be made project-specific and contain the appropriate detail for the appropriate level of involvement.

The matrix given in Part Four of this book (Chapter 9) is not intended to be a detailed procedures manual. Instead, it is a checklist for project managers and planners while they are establishing the deliverables and their requirements. These form the basis for quality of each typical activity that would need to be addressed during a project to ensure its success. It must be stressed that many projects will not involve each activity listed in each phase of this matrix, but that the project management team will have to decide at as early a stage as possible which activities are applicable to the project.

The deliverables and their requirements are fundamental to the drafting of the scope of the project. This is one of the cornerstones of a project, and it must be in place before the contractual phase can be started. The book will also illustrate the role that quality principles play in the important project management aspects of development and design, planning and cost engineering.

Scope

This work applies to the management for quality and the management of quality in projects from the earliest market need and conceptual phases, to the ultimate commissioning and, if applicable, decommissioning of a facility or plant that has been established by means of a given project. It is intended to provide guidance for project managers on quality matters and tools. The details and level of these discussions are aimed at giving enough insight into quality matters so that the broad management of the project can grasp the principles and be comfortable with their applicability as management and control tools during the various phases and in the case of various activities in the course of a project.

The project quality manager or person responsible for facilitating, promoting and advising on quality-related aspects of the project should be thoroughly conversant with these skills and disciplines. In the case of large projects, it is unlikely that the project quality manager will be an expert in all of these technologies. He/she will probably have to make use of contracted skills and expertise for several of the specific quality-related technologies.

The very nature of many projects will also require that many of these technologies, such as non-destructive examination or pressure vessel inspection, be contracted out to competent firms. The reason for this is that building up and maintaining such a capability in-house is costly, and such a capability cannot then be fully and economically utilized after the completion of the project.

This book is not intended to be a comprehensive treatise on these subjects, since many authoritative books have already been written on most of them. Any person requiring more detailed information or greater insight into these topics is referred to the list of suggested reading matter given at the end of the book.

The store of knowledge concerning quality has expanded so rapidly in the past 30 years that it would form a comprehensive library consisting of many hundreds of books and many thousands of articles. The suggested reading list is, therefore, only a small part of the total body of available knowledge on the subject. Should more information of a very specific nature be required, the reader would be advised to consult the national libraries or the major quality promoting institutions or universities. Some of the better-known of these are the American Society for Quality, the European Organization for Quality, the Japan Union of Scientists and Engineers, the University of Manchester, and the Massachusetts Institute of Technology.

The application of the principles of total management for quality to the fields of cost and time management is also included in the document so that its credibility and usefulness can be expanded accordingly. The systematic breakdown of the project into phases (Part 4) can also be applied to cost engineering and project planning as a useful checklist that will facilitate the ease and completeness with which these activities can be accomplished.

It is important that each activity be reviewed for applicability. Only applicable activities and involved parties on the matrix should be examined and converted from the generic terms of the matrix to those that are project-specific. However, this system is intended to apply to the stages and activities of the various phases of a project, as well as to the involved parties.

CHAPTER TWO

Quality philosophies and principles in projects

Introduction

The concepts 'quality principles' and 'quality philosophies' are often new and foreign to readers, and although many instinctively feel that they have a clear understanding of what quality is, they very often find that their instincts disappoint them.

It is also an unfortunate fact that many meetings and discussions on quality often end in confusion because the participants do not fully understand the terminology and nuances used by the various practitioners of this discipline, nor their implications. Therefore, in quality studies as in many other disciplines, while superficially there appears to be commonality of language usage, different people are in fact using different 'quality dialects' and this in itself causes problems and confusion.

This chapter, which deals with the philosophies and principles of quality in projects, will help to focus the reader's mind on the subject, in order to obtain clarity before continuing with this book.

Quality means different things to different people, depending upon their point of view. A businessman or businesswoman looks at quality to assess its possible contribution to customer and, more recently, to stakeholder satisfaction, to increased market share and ultimately to increased turnover and profitability. If quality fails to contribute towards meeting these needs, it starts to lose its lustre for the business person.

The consumer or user of the product or service looks at quality from a value-for-money viewpoint, and this includes acceptable useful life, ease of use, reliability and maintainability (where applicable) as well as cost and effort of ownership.

The quality practitioner views quality in terms of its ISO definition and in terms of what quality can do to further his/her career. The quality practitioner asks how it contributes towards meeting his/her personal needs in terms of material items and career satisfaction.

In a project, quality usually implies the supplying of facilities and services on time and within budget. Such facilities and services must conform to the project scope and specifications, and must be fit for their purpose, as defined in the contract. Quality is all about meeting the needs of customers and stakeholders. Their satisfaction is one of the major requirements to ensure the success of any business, organization or project – both now and in the future. Satisfied and happy customers base these positive feelings not only on the results of deliverables, whether products or services, but also on their perception of excellence and customer care.

Customers can only be happy when their needs have been fully met in terms of acceptable deliverables that are timeously available at an acceptable price and in acceptable quantities. An acceptable deliverable includes not only the as-received functional commissioned product or service, but also the total life-cycle, cost and convenience or inconvenience of ownership and use. Quality is therefore inextricably linked with reliability and maintainability. These factors are often not taken into account properly because the other project parameters of cost and time limitations dominate during the design, construction and commissioning phases of a project.

The customers' and stakeholders' needs and the deliverables (both products and services) that will satisfy these needs are seldom obvious. The customers' and stakeholders' needs have to be thoroughly discussed and understood by the service and product supplying parties, as well as by the customers and stakeholders themselves. This is all part of the process of converting customer and stakeholder perceptions into realizable reality. Only when such needs have been fully understood and accepted by all parties concerned can suitable deliverables be negotiated. 'Deliverables' in this case means product and service, which when used by the customer will satisfy given needs, without negating the rights and opportunities of others or the environment.

The agreed deliverables still have to be quantified in terms of the requirements that describe them, and the specifications and standards that make their production or realization possible. All of these must also be established, negotiated and mutually agreed upon so that the ultimate images in the minds of customers, stakeholders and suppliers or project managers are as close to reality as possible. This is not a 'once off' process, but often has to take place many times (especially in the case of large projects) to ensure continued acceptability between the customers and stakeholders on the one hand, and the supplier or project management on the other.

Quality can therefore be regarded as satisfying customers' and stakeholders' needs by means of sufficient mutually agreed deliverables that meet all the agreed requirements and specifications every time, on time and in an affordable manner. A succinct definition of quality in projects is: 'Meeting the requirements of the deliverables that satisfy the needs which have been identified and mutually agreed upon by the customers, stakeholders and the contractors.'

In ISO 8402 (1994) the International Organization for Standardization defines quality as 'the totality of characteristics of an entity that bear on its ability to satisfy stated or implied needs.' (Deming, 1982.) As an analysis of its key words shows, this definition neatly packages all the various aspects that have been discussed in this chapter.

During research on this subject, the author felt it would be wise to first examine the common usage and definitions, as found in the Oxford dictionary, of the words 'principles' and 'philosophy'. For the purposes of this book, these can be defined as follows:

Principle: Fundamental truth which forms the basis of reasoning and which can serve as a guide to action.

Philosophy: Love of wisdom or knowledge of that which deals with the ultimate reality or with the most general causes and principles of things.

An examination of the meanings of these two words makes the parallels self-evident. However, for ease of understanding, the philosophies pertaining to quality will be discussed first and thereafter the underlying principles. As can be seen from the definition of 'philosophy', 'principle' would seem to be a sub-set thereof. Another word requiring definition is that of 'project'.

The ISO/CD 10006 (1995) document, which is currently in committee draft (CD) form, defines 'project' as follows: 'Unique process consisting of a set of co-ordinated and controlled activities with start and finish dates undertaken to achieve an objective conforming to specific requirements including the constraints of time, cost and resources.'

In our view, the essence of this definition of 'project' is 'a series of activities to effect change in a planned and controlled manner for a specific end result, having finite commencement and conclusion dates, as well as finite resources'.

Philosophy of quality

Quality is a 'people business'

The underlying truth about quality is that it revolves around people and satisfying their perceived needs. Without people and needs, quality has no meaning and ceases to exist.

Because it is a 'people business' and refers to people's needs, quality cannot be divorced from the perceptual facets of how people see it. Therefore, quality also implies people's perception of having their needs met. Hence we are dealing here with the science of making people (customers and stakeholders) feel satisfied or happy through the goods, services, plant and equipment which can satisfy their needs. The holistic approach also requires that other forms of life still be sustainable after completion of the project and during operation of the facility.

Quality, therefore, cannot be divorced from the emotions of the receiver of the items or the service, as well as of those directly affected. When the project is examined in its totality, the giver of the item or the service must also be included. When projects are considered, the receiver is usually an organization or company. However, the organization or company consists of people who must operate the facility, ensuring that it is both viable and profitable, and remains that way.

Quality, because it revolves around meeting people's needs, seldom or virtually never occurs by chance. Meeting people's needs has become a carefully planned science, which means that quality is always the product of careful thought, effort and planning. Quality will never come into being spontaneously.

The paradigm shift for management

Management is the art and science of enabling people to achieve desired results by the use of their intelligence, skills, enthusiasm (including positive emotion) and resources. Management is also about managing change, which is the essence of a project. Kanter et al (1992) state that implementors managing change must not only be concerned about changing 'from what . . . to what', but that the path of progress cannot simply be determined by the destination. This discipline must be approached in a holistic way in order to achieve a balanced, successful result which can be sustained. Short-term flash-in-the-pan quarterly profit results should not be associated with a successful or even acceptable management style.

Management must first focus on 'doing the right things' and only then on doing things right. As the project progresses, these issues will have to be revisited so that, where necessary, course corrections can be made.

The indicators of successful management (doing the right things) are the following:

- A satisfied corps of customers that not only ensures return business, but also acts as an effective advertisement which brings in new business.

- A profitable organization that pays acceptable dividends to its shareholders (who are also stakeholders) as well as 'motivational bonuses' to its employees, and contributes towards the upliftment or empowerment of those communities directly affected by its activities.

- The conducting of business in such a manner that there is no unnatural deterioration in the health of its employees or of people and/or other life forms in the vicinity or areas affected by the facility or project.

- The conducting of business in a sustainable manner that will offer market stability and continuity to its customers, as well as job satisfaction and career opportunities to its employees. This concept also includes the avoidance of loss and waste, as well as obtaining optimum productive life out of its facilities and plant.

- The management of the project in such a way that the contracts of temporary workers are fair and clear yet cost-effective.

The true entrepreneur

Any form of entrepreneurial endeavour is aimed at improving the lot of (usually) humans, although nowadays more and more other life forms are included as well. If any endeavour (project) is to be sustainable, tolerable and meaningful, it cannot be to the detriment of others, nor can it exclude them. Any entrepreneurial activity or intervention such as a project will disturb an existing situation. It is important to ensure that the disturbance can be forecasted, accurately minimized and tolerated by people and other life forms who are influenced either directly or indirectly.

If this is to happen successfully and sustainably, the effort has to be carefully managed in order to obtain the correct results. This is applicable to any project, the result of which must deliver a product, service or system which will give acceptable results. The process of carrying out a project must also be managed in such a way that the total cost of achieving the end result is not greater than the value of the result to the customers. Customers can be immediate, intermediate or final stakeholders, society or its environment and surroundings.

It is always important to ensure that the desired end result is not confused with the process itself. The management approach needed during the process of achieving a result can often differ considerably from the end result itself and how it should be managed in the future.

By means of a management system any good entrepreneur should, in a sustainable manner, be able to achieve the following as the product of good management:

- customer satisfaction (at all levels of involvement);

- profitability (rather than quarterly smash-and-grab);

- stakeholder satisfaction;

- avoidance of loss or opportunity of loss;

- avoidance of unnatural deterioration of health or loss of life of all affected directly or indirectly (safety and health);

- avoidance of operating at the unacceptable expense of life in any form (the environment).

The real process of management – satisfying reasonable needs

The above-mentioned can be summarized in the flow-chart of events (Fig 2.1) that the manager must manage in order to stay in business profitably and sustainably.

This flow-chart is an expansion of the 'all-work-is-a-process' principle discussed by Crosby (1979). The input to this flow-chart is traced back to basic human needs, and even to the needs of other life forms. The output of the chart also takes cognizance of the fact that all processes have both desirable and undesirable outputs, and both of these influence the satisfaction of customers and stakeholders.

If any product or service resulting from entrepreneurial effort does not satisfy the needs of humans and even the broader needs of life in

FIGURE 2.1 Holistic management for sustainable success

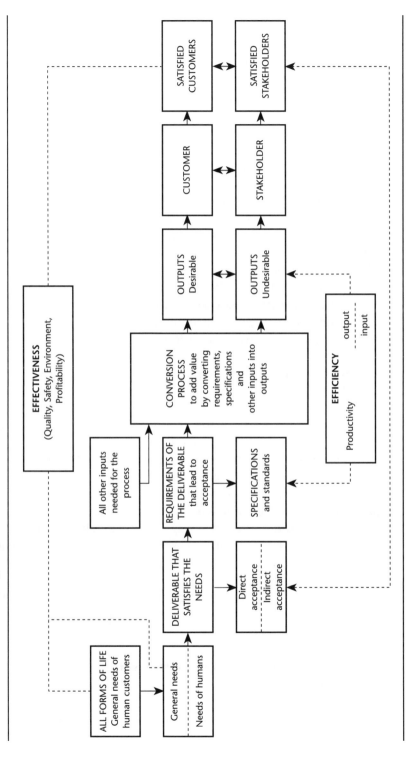

general, it will be short-lived, no matter how well the rest of the internal operations are managed. The product of good management is the satisfaction of a broad spectrum of needs, be they direct (and marketable as a product or service), or indirect (which can be very important to the people and other life forms affected).

Effective management starts when the real needs are determined, together with the deliverables, namely the goods, systems and services that will satisfy these needs. The deliverables must be quantified in terms of requirements and specifications which will make their correct realization or production possible. These form the governing input into the activities and processes that are needed to achieve the desired result. Other inputs that are needed to serve the process, such as people, resources, energy, funds, etc. must also be optimized and managed.

Every process has desirable but also undesirable outputs. Both of these must be managed in order to increase the desirable aspects and decrease the undesirable ones. The ratio of the value of desirable outputs over the cost of undesirable outputs must always be positive. As soon as the cost of the undesirable outputs outweighs the value of the desirable outputs, the project or activity is no longer of value to society. In this context, cost and value must first of all be expressed in monetary terms, but may not be limited to these terms. In many instances, the aesthetics of natural beauty, uniqueness or rareness of a particular environment and its life forms will have to be taken into account, as will indirect health hazards to the people living in the vicinity of the facility, or who are affected by a by-product (undesirable output).

It is management's responsibility in the 'do-the-right-things' phase to establish what the undesirable outputs are, quantify the total costs (both direct and indirect) and either eliminate them, manage them acceptably, or convert them into a desirable output, such as finding a use for a by-product and thus converting it into a saleable item. Any endeavour that does not take all of these factors into account is usually short-lived: either the stakeholders will shut the facility down by protesting, or they will influence the customer to shut it down by withholding support (or both). A holistic approach to management is the only sustainable way in which success can be achieved.

Continuous improvement – a key element for achieving quality

The modern-day world in which we live has conditioned us not to accept things that go wrong and to express our dissatisfaction. As a result, mankind has come to accept an approach that the best services, goods and facilities or plants of today will barely meet the minimum acceptable standards of tomorrow. In other words, we find ourselves living in a world that demands continuous improvement.

Continuous improvement has been a key role-player in mankind's progress throughout the ages. History has shown that societies where improvement has not been permitted, or has even been deliberately hindered, become backward and can even become extinct. Projects and project management are no exception to this rule. The progress that has been made in the development of new skills, processes and equipment that facilitate the project process is impressive. This becomes very evident when certain historic accounts of projects, especially those in the field of construction, are studied.

Nor are the management processes necessary in order to achieve customer and stakeholder satisfaction (quality) on projects an exception. These processes, because they are more abstract and the deliverables more difficult to define in terms of tangible items, are less obvious and have to be thought through very carefully.

The management process cannot be tackled in a haphazard manner as the 'flavour of the month'. It will usually involve the project management team, and where such a team has been established as a professional project management group that handles many projects, the quality improvement process and principles can span more than one project. In cases where a project team has been assembled to tackle a single project and will then be disbanded, the improvement process will be very difficult or even impossible to achieve. There are, however, many principles in the improvement process that can still be applied successfully to individual projects which have a relatively short time-span of 6 to 24 months.

J M Juran et al (1979) advocate project-by-project quality improvement. This approach (which has been used successfully for many years) recommends identifying problems in an organization and then assembling a project team from within the organization. This team will consist of those affected by the problem, as well as suitably skilled people, who will tackle the solving of this problem as a project. This is usually carried out as an additional task, although in some instances the problem may require urgent attention and it will become a specific task. At the conclusion of this project (possibly extensive but more probably small), the project team is disbanded and its members continue with their normal functions and duties.

David Hutchins (1992) developed an improvement 'road map' project, shown in Figure 2.2 (with acknowledgement to David Hutchins International).

FIGURE 2.2 Project by project improvement

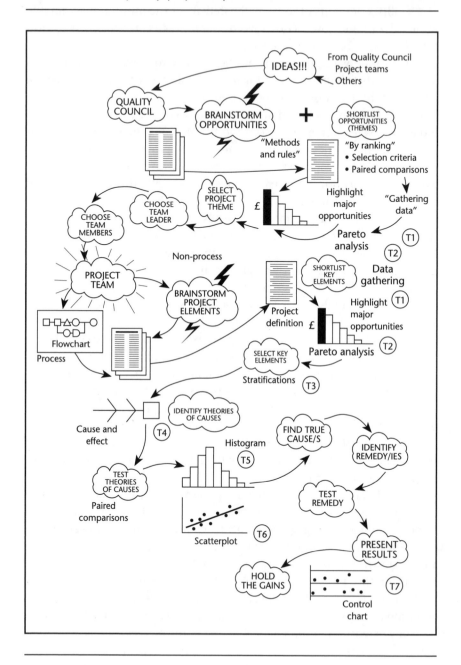

Careful study of Figure 2.2 will indicate that there are five basic steps in the improvement project road map, namely to:

- understand;

- aim;

- focus;

- theorize;

- establish dominant causes.

These are all steps that have to be carried out in order to establish and fully understand the nature of the problem. These steps must precede any attempt at finding a remedy. This also illustrates the importance and value of the up-front thinking, research and planning that must be put into the improvement process before the implementation of the best remedy can be attempted.

Boaden and Dale (1994) have developed a generic framework for managing quality improvement. This is illustrated in Table 2.1 and Figure 2.3. This framework requires a broad-based, company-wide approach, although in an organization it will be started on a pilot scale. This process must also be accompanied by a change in the organization's culture. Once again, one of the key concepts is up-front planning and preparation, coupled with visible management commitment and staying power, or, as one chief executive put it, 'sticktoitiveness'.

Quality as a life-long feature

Another fundamental truth about quality is that the bitterness of poor quality lives long after the sweetness of cheap price or timeous delivery has been forgotten. This is especially true of plants or facilities that are created through projects. The term 'quality' also embraces other derivatives which are time-based, namely reliability, which means or implies the ability to be operated and satisfy the customer's needs for a long period of time, or at least for a specified or perceptually acceptable period of time.

Quality also encompasses serviceability, which is the ability to keep the item or service both usable and in peak performance by means of periodic corrections and improvement. A further important quality concept is maintainability, which implies the ease with which the deliverable can be maintained without costing the owner or customer too much in terms of money, time or inconvenience.

TABLE 2.1 Quality improvement framework: A summary

Organizing	Systems and Techniques	Measurement and Feedback	Changing the Culture
Formulation of a clear LONG-TERM STRATEGY for the process of quality improvement, integrated with other key business strategies, departmental policies, and objectives	Identification of the TOOLS AND TECHNIQUES applicable to different stages of the process of quality improvement	Identification and definition of key INTERNAL AND EXTERNAL PERFORMANCE MEASURES to assess the progress being made and to ensure customer satisfaction	Development of an assessment of the CURRENT STATUS of organizational culture, before developing and implementing plans for change
Definition and communication of a COMMON ORGANIZATIONAL DEFINITION OF QUALITY, TQM, AND QUALITY IMPROVEMENT after discussion	Development of the appropriate type of TRAINING in the use of tools and techniques, targeted at the right people	DISCUSSION WITH CUSTOMERS about expected performance, needs, and expectations, using a variety of techniques	Recognition of the ONGOING NATURE OF CULTURE CHANGE, rather than a prerequisite for TQM
Selection of an APPROACH TO TQM	Consideration of the use of a formal QUALITY SYSTEM, if one is not in place	Consideration of BENCH-MARKING, once the organization has taken some steps to improve quality	The development of PLANS FOR CHANGE that enable it to take place in a consistent and incremental manner
Identification of the organizations and people (internal and external) who can be SOURCES OF ADVICE on aspects of TQM	Identification and implementation of OTHER SYSTEMS AND STANDARDS that may be required by customers, legislation, or in order to compete	Consideration of various means for CELEBRATION AND COMMUNICATION OF SUCCESS, and the development of methods for recognizing the efforts of teams and individuals	The recognition of THE ROLE OF PEOPLE within the organization
Identification of STAGES OF IM-PROVEMENT activity, taking into account the starting point of the organization, the motivation for qual-ity improvement, and the tools that may be applicable	Adoption of PROCESS ANALYSIS AND IMPROVEMENT as a continual part of the organization's quality improvement process	Consideration of LINKING REWARDS TO QUALITY IMPROVEMENT ACTIVITIES AND RESULTS	Identification of the INTER-RELATIONSHIPS OF ALL ACTIVITIES, and the way in which they contribute to quality of service and product within the organization in order to minimize conflict

TABLE 2.1 *Continued*

Organizing	Systems and Techniques	Measurement and Feedback	Changing the Culture
Recognition of EXECUTIVE LEADERSHIP, TANGIBLE COMMITMENT, AND SUPPORT as being crucial at all stages		Utilization of some means of ASSESSING THE PROGRESS TOWARD WORLD-CLASS PERFORMANCE	Identification of FACTORS THAT INDICATE THAT TQM HAS STARTED TO CHANGE CULTURE
Development and communication of VISION AND MISSION STATEMENTS that are concise and understandable to all employees			Consideration of the CULTURE OF A COUNTRY AND ITS PEOPLE in planning for change
Establishment of a formal program of EDUCATION AND TRAINING			
Establishment of an ORGANIZATIONAL INFRASTRUCTURE that will ultimately facilitate local ownership of quality improvement			
Establishment of TEAMWORK that is designed to become part of the organization's method of working			

Source: Reproduced with kind permission of Prentice Hall International (UK) Ltd. based on Table 5.1, page 130 of *Managing Quality* edited by Barrie G Dale, 2nd edition, 1994

For example, if a product which satisfies a specific need has very high maintenance or other ownership cost (such as a high risk of loss) and if it necessitates high insurance or maintenance costs, a customer may decide to look for an alternative which is more affordable. In extreme cases, he/she may even forgo satisfying the need. Quality is therefore not an absolute concept that can stand alone in its own right. It is the result or product of all the correctly managed activities, items or

FIGURE 2.3 The quality improvement framework

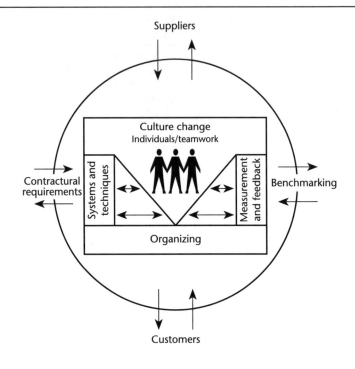

services needed to give (or establish) one end result, be it an item, a service or plant or a facility.

Principles

It is now necessary to discuss some of the quality concepts and some of the misconceptions that are currently prevalent. Most of these perceptions can be traced back to circumstances prevailing at a particular time which influenced the lives of many people. The following are some of the more commonly held ideas about the concept of quality.

Quality is reflected in the exterior finish

This belief is dying out, but had its roots in the pre-industrial era when most items were produced by craftsmen, and each order that was placed was different and a project in its own right. A study of any of the well-restored equipment or even tools in a museum such as the one in Birmingham (UK) will show that a great deal of effort was put into decorating such items ornately. Polished copper and brass were also used to improve the aesthetic appeal of the exterior of the equipment. The development of chrome plating further enhanced this style, and its use in automobiles – with relatively few improvements to the functional features or efficiency of the car in the late 1940s and 1950s – is evidence of this perception.

Today many discerning customers look beyond the external appearance of finish (and even regard excessively ornate finishes with suspicion). Provided that the item is neat and aesthetically acceptable, customers are more interested in the value of the product or service for them personally.

Quality as meeting specifications

The advent of the Taylor approach to industrialization also meant the virtual demise of what the author prefers to call the 'manufacturing craftsman'. The 'artistic craftsman/woman' still exists and thrives today, but is usually engaged for the impact of appearance and aesthetic reasons, rather than for the functionality of the item produced. The disappearance of personal skill and pride taken in 'crafted quality' means that this vacuum has had to be filled by something else in order to arrive at an acceptable product or service.

The 'something else' was a more technical description of what, in the opinion of the designer and/or manufacturer, has to be achieved. The general level of education during the early industrialized period was poor. Specifications were drawn up by those few who were deemed to be knowledgeable, and were generally accepted by the masses as being the 'best for them' in a parochial manner. The first specifications rarely took cognizance of what the customer or even stakeholder required, and concentrated more on design and fabrication than on customer satisfaction and safety. Compliance with a correctly drafted specification is a very important aspect, but it is only one part of the whole chain of events needed to achieve quality.

Fitness for purpose

This concept was put forward by Dr W Edward Deming (1982) in the early 1950s. Private discussions that the author has had with Dr Deming indicate that the mind-set of quality being fitness for purpose had its roots in the logistical requirements of the Second World War.

The ability of a country to produce, in sufficient quantities, weapons and munitions that 'did the job, every time' placed it at an advantage over its enemies, especially if their munitions were not always reliable. The Allied forces were painfully aware of this fact because they entered the war at a disadvantage in terms of readiness relative to the Axis forces. In many spheres, the Allied weaponry was not able to 'do the job' when it had to face the might of superior Axis weapons. This helped to promote the 'fitness for purpose' concept.

The Depression and the Second World War created a massive backlog in durable consumer products. The demand for these products meant that companies in the 1950s and 1960s could produce almost any product that worked and was fit for the purpose, and the product-hungry market would gobble it up.

Quality as 'fitness for purpose' was the natural result of these times. It is also a fundamental fact that no customer is prepared to pay for a product or service that is not fit for purpose, and in this respect fitness for purpose is one of the prerequisites for quality.

Compliance with requirements

This concept was popularized by Philip Crosby (1979) and is one of his four fundamentals of quality. The concept is based on the psychological perception that quality is in the mind of customers, and that what they expect of a product or service needs to be quantified in terms of requirements. Customer satisfaction should result from systematic compliance with such correctly quantified requirements.

The concept considers not only the final customer, but also the chain of internal or intermediate customers who have requirements that have to be met in order to comply with the ultimate requirements of the final customer. This approach to quality is a far more holistic one, and looks at the entire set of events leading to customer satisfaction. It also emphasizes that each link in the chain is important, and failure to satisfy the requirements of a single customer link will lead to failure of the entire chain.

Giving users what they want

This concept focuses on the end user and takes cognizance of specific wants. It shifts the emphasis to the user and recognizes that his/her wants are paramount. This reflects a more modern approach in a world where there is sufficient manufacturing or production capacity to satisfy (or even saturate) the global market for a particular product. This approach takes the highly competitive nature of business today into account: those who satisfy the customer's perceived needs will get the customer's business. However, this approach does not always take note of the stakeholders' wants and needs. Very often the longer term view is not taken, and this can result in a negative impact on the long-term situation.

Project managers often fall into the trap of only giving customers what 'they' want and consequently running into trouble with stakeholders and facility operators and maintainers. This can have a very negative impact on the ultimate profitability and viability of the project deliverable, as well as on the reputation of the contractor.

This approach often does not take into account the negative aspects of the process of establishing the product or service that satisfied the need, which can lead to a negative result.

Giving users what they need

This is very similar to giving users what they want, but it does take a longer term view. The supplier of the product or service will not only establish the immediate want but will also look further to other needs that are related to it. These needs may include reliability, maintainability, safety, updating and even longer term investment or re-sale value.

This is a more holistic approach. These needs are carefully and mutually agreed upon and quantified in terms of deliverables, their requirements and specifications. This concept starts to take a broader approach to total quality. Unfortunately, it often does not take into account the needs of the stakeholders or the intermediate users. This omission can have very serious consequences for total quality, i.e. both customer and stakeholder satisfaction. This approach must therefore also be seen as only part of the whole quality picture.

Quality as value for money

This concept of quality is usually the point of view of the end-user or consumer. This is particularly true in cases where the end-user has little influence over the quality of the product or service while it is being produced. It usually applies to instances where a variety of suitable or at least usable products are on offer and the customer must weigh up his/her needs, requirements and resources against what is being offered. In many instances, none of the products are an ideal match for the customer's needs, and the customer must choose the best *affordable* option. Brand names or approval by standards authorities or other quality reviewing organizations can play an important role in helping the customer to make up his or her mind.

When products or services are purchased under such conditions, customers often take a product life-cycle point of view, and require affordable serviceability and product reliability, as well as an affordable purchase price. Under these circumstances, customers are ignorant of the total chain of events that led to their receiving the acceptable product. On the other hand, they are very conscious of after-sales service, which affects them directly. Should customers become aware of negative events in the production chain either from a product or stakeholder's point of view, they are able to sanction it by withholding their purchasing power.

While this is also a valid point of view, it does not take the whole quality picture into account, and in turn it is only a part of the whole issue of total quality.

It is clear from this discussion that all of these perceptions have a place in the total quality concept, but that they are only part of a far greater whole which needs to be approached and managed in a holistic way. The tables given in the last section of this book attempt to provide the reader with a set of 'memory joggers' pertaining to most of the major items that should be taken into account when managing a project. In this way, a more acceptable, broadly based result may be achieved.

Action guides

The fundamentals which can be used as a basis of reasoning and as a guide for action, concerning quality that results from this philosophy, are the next topic for discussion.

If we accept that quality basically revolves around satisfying the needs of people and organizations, then we have to define it more clearly and in more usable terms so that anybody who delivers goods or services will be able to satisfy their customers' needs in full. In principle, therefore, quality becomes fitness-for-use and more customer-specific. The ability to produce services and products that continue to satisfy customers' needs by meeting their requirements can be seen as true quality.

A fundamental truth that flows out of this is that quality does not happen by chance at the end of the process. It comes about in a very planned, orderly and controlled manner throughout the process of establishing and delivering a plant facility, product or service. Each step, from the earliest stage of establishing what the customer's needs and requirements are, right to delivering the ultimate plant product or service is important. Quality involves a whole chain of activities: each activity is a link in its own right and each link has its own output or deliverable which affects quality. In turn, each has its own requirements, and flowing out of these requirements is the activity output or deliverables which conform to the requirements for the next step in the process. In this way, a whole chain consisting of acceptable links for quality is created.

It is essential, therefore, that all the sub-requirements and sub-deliverables add up to a total, ultimate requirement and deliverable that will satisfy the customer or facility owner. Customers do not pay for requirements; they pay for output or deliverables in the form of goods and services. Therefore, requirements must adequately describe deliverables and the deliverables must conform to these requirements. These will bring about the deliverables which a customer pays for in order to have a specific need satisfied.

Another important principle regarding quality is that quality cannot be approached in an *ad hoc* manner. Achieving an unbroken chain of events with the deliverables being correct for every link or activity, requires that getting things right (quality) must be approached and managed in a systematic and planned manner. Quality has to be planned up-front. The plans have to be carefully reviewed to detect potential errors, and they must be approved, executed, measured and controlled. This must happen progressively as the process of 'creating' the facility or service takes its course. Errors, as well as methods of doing things better, will become apparent as the project progresses. These factors will often have to be evaluated carefully in order to avoid errors and improve or correct the system and/or the 'tools' that support the system. This system must translate or change a whole range of inputs, such as materials, equipment, energy, knowledge, skills, specific training, environment, buildings and workshops, etc., into the desired end result which is a product or service.

Quality is not an absolute concept in itself, but rather the product of a competently managed system and process. In the minds and hands of trained and motivated people, such a system can be correctly utilized to convert all the inputs into facilities, products or services that meet perceived needs with the minimum tolerable level of undesirable output, cost-effectively and timeously.

Products or services often create a direct product, a related product or service and a waste product. For example, if you buy a plant, its functionality is the direct product, but the off-sites, utilities and functional services, i.e. water, roads, security, fencing, are also important and have a bearing on the plant's functionality and the quality of the total, final project. The waste from the project, i.e. soil from earthworks, left-over concrete, damaged or lost material, etc., can also have a negative effect on quality.

There are other quality-related factors that feature in a project, such as the data and information handling systems, the management of the position status and location (i.e. configuration) of key documents (and equipment) such as drawings, contracts, specifications, etc. Many companies and organizations have even found themselves in a quality 'revolutionary' situation. For example, this can occur when faced with major contracts in which the customers bluntly stipulate that unless a formal quality system and verification method exist in the company, the company would not be considered for the order. In such cases, crash programmes have had to be instituted to address this deficiency in order to be considered for the project.

However, such window-dressing cases are usually short-lived and do not produce the desired results because the technical and systematic introduction of quality has not gone hand-in-hand with awareness of human factors such as a 'right first time' work ethic, pride and enthusiasm for performing the work correctly every time. The importance of systematic quality and adherence to these systems has also not been emphasized.

An important basic principle of quality is that while technical aspects and systems have to be addressed, the human side of quality often plays an even more important role. The human side must be seen as not only valuable to the people in the organization using it, but also as a method of ridding people's lives of wasted effort and unnecessary hassle, and of improving the effectiveness of their work. Furthermore it must be seen as a method of making sure that the people do the right things correctly, thereby enhancing pride in workmanship and achievement of the project.

Because quality requires people to establish and maintain it, the systems approach and all the technical tools for quality have to be supported by a humanistic approach. Important fundamentals, such as 'people can only provide their customers with the quality they in turn receive from their management', have to be understood by management. A gradual evolution of the importance of these principles has to be grasped by all and used actively.

Management is the catalyst, initiator and enabler for doing things correctly (the quality process). Workers are the true vehicles through which it becomes a reality in terms of goods and services, and ultimately a successfully completed project. However, an underlying truth is that the root cause of 80 per cent of problems with quality lies in management's style and decisions. The remaining 20 per cent are due to workers and staff. These are usually experienced as hassles, inefficient facilities, training, scope or specification changes and other human-related causes, such as a lack of quality awareness. These problems can only be corrected through education and training, which can help instill a pro-quality attitude, culture and work ethic.

PART TWO

Key elements affecting quality in projects

CHAPTER THREE

The application of quality management principles to project planning

Introduction

Quality almost never happens by accident. It is always the result of careful thought, planning, preparation and execution. If quality is not pro-actively planned into a project then partial quality is the best result that can occur.

> Project planning is the managerial tool that is used to achieve systematic and optimum use of resources in order to achieve a particular objective within limited time and resources (a project).

It is only possible to use resources effectively when the objectives of a project and their inter-relationships are clearly understood. Oberlender (1993) states that 'project planning is the heart of good project management because it provides the central communication that co-ordinates the work of all parties. Planning also establishes the *benchmark* for the project control system to track the quantity, cost and timing of the work required to successfully complete the project.'

It is during the planning phase that the desired results, as specified by the design in terms of acceptable deliverables that will make the project a success, namely quality, must also be planned into the project. If the planning of the project does not include the quality aspects then an incomplete benchmark or reference point will be established and the central communication function will also be incomplete.

It therefore follows that the control system that must track quantity, cost and time will be incomplete if the aspects that govern success are not also related to deliverables and milestones. The coupling of success factors to milestones is necessary so that criteria are set to indicate when a task has been (satisfactorily) completed. One of these criteria set is quality to help to avoid wasted effort, in terms of the time and cost that have to be expended in order to correct problems. A good project planning system also has mechanisms built into it that will highlight deviations from the original plan, and will allow for corrective steps to be formulated and taken timeously.

Planning must also create opportunities and sufficient time on the schedule for:

- bringing personnel up to speed on the project;

- training in new or improved techniques;

- the exchange of information between the various parties on the project;

- time to perform reviews and formally approve key steps, procedures and activities on the project;

- the creation and operation of management systems that are project specific, such as information capturing, handling, storage and dissemination.

In this chapter, planning and scheduling must not be confused. Planning involves a holistic managerial approach to effective utilization of all resources, whereas scheduling is a subset of planning and usually involves the sequence and time requirements to complete the activities that comprise the project.

The holistic approach to planning usually requires that the following key issues be taken into account:

- What are the major elements or 'deliverables' and their specifications of the project?

- Who is responsible for getting the work done?

- What physical resources (including services) are required and available?

- What information will be needed to conceptualize, manage and control the project?

- What human resources are needed and are available?

- What financial resources are needed and are available?

- What systems will be needed to manage the project?

All of these issues have a direct bearing on the intermediate and the final 'project customers'. The correct handling of each of these means that, in their own way, they will contribute to the overall success of the project. Each of these aspects will have to deliver specific results (deliverables) in order to satisfy a specific project need, which, by its nature, will have specific requirements and specifications for success or acceptability (i.e. quality). The project need directly or indirectly influences the deliverables and consequently influences the planning of a project.

Oberlender (1993) lists the 12 desired results of project planning, i.e. quality determinants of a successful project planning programme, as follows:

- Finish the project on time.

- Continuous (uninterrupted) flow of work (no delays).

- Reduced amount of rework (least amount of changes).

- Minimize confusion and misunderstanding.

- Increased knowledge of status of project by everyone.

- Meaningful and timely reports to management.

- You run the project instead of the project running you.

- Knowledge of scheduled times of key parts of the project.

- Knowledge of distribution of costs of the project.

- Accountability of people, defined responsibility and authority.

- Clear understanding of who does what, when and how much.

- Integration of all work to ensure a fault-free project for the owner.

The author would suggest that the following be added to complete the list from a quality point of view.

- A full list of all the deliverables required to complete the project.

- A full list of all the requirements needed to describe the deliverables.

- The success factors and handover acceptability of each milestone in the project.

It is also necessary for the planning group to develop parameters and methods of reassessing these 15 aspects as they form the basis of determining whether the project planning is taking place successfully or not. It is very important to measure this success because of the role that planning plays in project management. Examples of measures of this success will be given in the section on Quality and project planning inputs and products of this chapter.

Early activities that affect the quality of planning

Initial activities

There are several activities that must occur at the beginning of the project preparation process if the planning and management of the project is to be successful. Failure to perform these steps successfully can have a major impact on the ultimate quality of the project if the nature and extent of these factors are not fully researched, understood and quantified *before* the final contracts are signed. The result of this omission will be that insufficient effort and resources will be planned and allocated, leading to problems and short cuts as the project progresses, in an attempt to meet agreed milestones at agreed costs. Experience has taught that short cuts always have a negative impact on quality. If quality is to be achieved on a project then these initial activities must be carefully carried out as the foundation on which sound planning is based. A little extra care expended on quality planning early in the project planning phase has been shown to save a lot of time in scheduling and execution, as well as money on re-work.

Kimmons (1990) identifies the activities that must occur at the beginning of the project preparation process as:

- scope definition;
- project objectives;
- identifying unique problems;
- selecting a strategy.

Haynes (1990) includes the concept of establishing a project objective and a basic strategy for achieving the objective as the first two planning steps. Haynes also includes the planning of the quality dimension in the early planning steps. He states that 'planning for quality requires attention to detail' and that 'the goal of quality planning is to ensure that the output of the project will perform – that it will do what it is supposed to do'. Setting quality criteria at an early stage ensures that project objectives can be met.

Engesser, in chapter 3 of *Project Management: A Reference for Professionals*, also includes project philosophy in these early activities of pre-planning, as this has a direct influence on the project scope and objectives.

Quality and scope definition

There are two aspects to be considered when defining what the project is supposed to do in the scope, and the quality effectiveness and accuracy of the scope definition process itself.

The first aspect requires that not only is the scope of the project defined, but that the requirements, measures and means that are necessary to successful completion form part of the scope. These can be used to monitor, measure and ultimately accept the finished project as being fully completed, and able to be handed over to the customer. These standards and the manner in which they are to be evaluated need to be negotiated between the project management and the customer, and should be included in the project contract as an integral part of the scope.

The second aspect (the scope definition process) concerns the effectiveness whereby the full scope is determined. The quality of the scope determination and definition process will also influence whether the issues have been successfully determined, or whether there are gaps in the process that will only become evident in a costly, time consuming manner as the project progresses.

The normal quality approach would be to use a matrix-organized team approach for scope determination and definition, including the customer, and where possible main contractors or sub-contractors. A further step in the quality discipline would be to have the scope, as defined, reviewed by a competent third party for gaps or areas that are not clearly defined and quantified. The method of definition must be clear and concise enough to be included in the project contract and be monitored and enforced by the contract. If the quality related aspects of a project are not included in the scope and the contract, they have in effect been 'contracted out' of the project and the customer will have to 'accept what they get' because they are powerless to enforce anything different after the contract has been agreed and signed.

The customer has the greatest leverage to achieve quality during the scope definition and contract negotiation phase. Thereafter their power and ability to influence quality diminishes as the process of project realization progresses.

The scope of work to be performed will usually embrace the following:

- facilities equipment and products to be acquired, installed and commissioned;

- services to be performed (and/or hired);

- documents to be produced that describe the criteria for successful achievement of the above, as well as those needed for contract close out and training for operation and maintenance of the final facility.

Kimmons (1990) lists the outline of a typical scope definition as follows:

- official identification of the project;

- a brief description of the project;

- pertinent contract data affecting the work to be done;

- licensing information/conditions/constraints.

It is also important that the responsibilities of the various parties be spelt out in the scope definition. Donald Engesser in Chapter 3 of *Project Management: A Reference for Professionals* (Marcel Dekker Inc, 1989) states that during scope definition: 'most key areas of project activity must be addressed, at least superficially, during this phase'. This makes sure that the quality aspects of the key areas also receive attention.

Quality and project objectives

Projects are undertaken in order to achieve some benefit to the customer, and to satisfy a specific need. If during the preparation and execution of the project these are not fully achieved then the project was unsuccessful or at best only partially successful. It is therefore necessary to establish, list and communicate the objectives to satisfy agreed customer needs to those who plan the work, as well as those who have to execute it. This activity is especially valuable to the customer as it helps focus attention on what has to be achieved.

There is often a perception that the project objectives are only complete if the project is on time and within budget. The quality aspects influence the life-cycle performance and longer term issues which will determine the ultimate success, namely that of successfully defining and meeting the objectives so that the project completion adds value to the customer while still being acceptable to the stakeholder and environment.

Project objectives should be prioritized into principal and major objectives so that the project manager can prioritize resources and effort accordingly. Some of the typical project objectives can be:

- a full description of the operating output parameters of the facility being established and quality of product or service produced;

- expected life of the facility;

- maintance frequencies and approach;

- safety and environmental conditions;

- budget and time constraints;

- the use of proven equipment and systems;

- level of operational costs of the facility

- use of specific sources of feed materials and suppliers of equipment and services.

The influence of project philosophy on quality

Most projects will be either driven or significantly influenced by fundamental philosophical aspects, be they directly formulated and stated in the contract, or in the minds of the project manager and work force. The latter often comes in the form of the 'mindset' of project management and is influenced by the broad approach of the project management organization, as well as experience on previous contracts or projects. These philosophies often have a profound effect on the approach to the project in general and quality in particular. If the mindset of the project management team is dominated by cost and schedule factors only, then quality will suffer and run a sad third place at the expense of customer satisfaction and long term success of the project.

Project philosophies can be many and varied and can be imposed by the customer, local authorities, specific safety and environmental requirements, the project manager, politicians, and the project management group themselves. It is essential that these philosophical issues be thrashed out before the contract is negotiated. These issues need to be brought into the open and where necessary included in the project contract. In many instances it will be necessary to iteratively re-visit the project scope and objectives in order to allow for these philosophical requirements and also to eliminate the opportunity for conflict, error, or unpleasant surprises as the project progresses.

Some of the typical philosophical issues to be considered include:

- desired return on investment;
- targeted operational service factors and maintenance approach;
- allowance for future expansion;
- participation by local industries and local content;
- technology transfer or developmental attitudes;
- use of local labour;
- involvement of local trade unions;
- social issues from the community;
- safety and health requirements of the operational facility as well as during the execution of the project;
- environmental issues;
- influence of local authorities and politics;
- use of benchmark projects to monitor project results.

This list is by no means comprehensive and the appropriate list for each project should be established at the beginning of the project during the scope determination phase. All these factors can have an influence on the quality of the final project, and on whether the customer and stakeholders will be satisfied or not.

The influence that each will have on quality, as well as schedule and budget, needs to be determined, quantified, and integrated into the planning process in a pro-active manner in order to ensure that they are dealt with competently.

Quality and project specific problems

Almost every major project will have certain specific problematic circumstances that will need to be pro-actively identified and addressed in the project planning process. Failure to identify these issues and their nature will inevitably lead to problems in fully meeting all the project objectives. This failure automatically means that the end result of the project, and consequently quality, will be compromised. This will also have a negative impact on project schedule and budget. Experience has taught that where this happens quality is usually compromised in order to solve the problem with the least impact on the schedule or the budget.

A problem that has been identified, studied, and defined usually ceases to be a problem, but becomes a series of tasks in the work breakdown structure. At this stage the emphasis must be on problem identification. It is more important to fully establish what these problems are than to solve them, as the solution phase will follow later.

The quality aspect at this stage relates to the thoroughness of identification of the problems or problem areas. The elegance of the solutions to the problems also impacts on the ultimate quality, but this forms part of the detail planning and design activities. Kimmons (1990) lists some categories that should be considered when searching out problems that are unique to a project, namely:

- *New technology*: Unproven processes where the objectives of the project are not open to accepting this risk.

- *Prototype equipment*: Sealed-up or nearly developed equipment presents an area of risk not compatible with projects demanding reliability of operation and maintenance.

- *Site conditions*: Unusual climates such as Arctic or desert conditions as well as challenges presented by outer space and the bottoms of oceans.

- *Limited resources*: A shortage of skilled technicians or labourers at a jobsite, the possibility of owner imposed restrictions on spending, limited space for the facilities with accompanying design and erection complications.

- *Delays in obtaining permits*: Start of construction or start of operations is dependent upon receiving the corresponding permits.

- *Process control systems*: Complications with the design procurement, installation and start up of very complex systems.

- *Difficult access*: No conventional transportation means to site.

- *Labour*: some areas have a history of labour turmoil threatening a prolonged construction period and poor productivity. Where labour contracts are expiring, renegotiation may cause delays.

- *Economic conditions*: High rates of escalation, the threat of suppliers' business failure, and uncertain markets may all create problems.

The author would like to add several more categories that can have an impact on quality, namely:

- *Greenfield project site*: Sites of this nature always have the potential for problems in terms of climate, geology and terrain access, as well as acceptability to the local population, etc.

- *Reliability of input data*: input data in the planning, design and even construction process is often extrapolated from other projects, or from preliminary site or demographic information which is not necessarily accurate, and will need to be independently verified by competent people or sources.

- *Local politics*: A significant project in an economically depressed area will inevitably arouse political interest in the possibilities that it presents for political scoring of 'brownie points'.

- *Special environmental considerations*: These can impose restrictions on both the project realization process and the process design that can have serious consequences.

- *Acceptability to the local community*: A project, process or ultimate product that will be unacceptable to the local community for environmental, ethical or religious reasons will have to be managed and the public carefully informed. The project site may even have to be relocated.

- *The potential for friction between contractor and client*: Channels are needed for honest, open, mature and frank communication between the contractor and the client.

Some of these issues may be obvious and merely need listing, but others often exist that are less easily identified, and it is those that need careful analysis to establish what they are, and what the extent of the problem is or could be. By using a thorough value analysis approach, each of these issues can be fully evaluated, broken down, checked, solutions generated and selected for optimal results.

It needs to be noted that such management related (quality) audits during this early stage could lead to the identification of one or more of these issues which may ultimately derail the project. Action at this early stage could be taken to redesign, change scope, locality, technology and strategy to ensure success or lead to an 'offramp' decision to shelve the project.

The full extent of customer and especially stakeholder problems where these consist of large groups of people are seldom obvious, and special care has to be taken to win them over to the project by up-front contact, openness, honesty, consultation and, later, continuous feedback. It is also advisable to keep all stakeholders fully informed as the project progresses, and specific feedback sessions will have to be planned into the project to achieve these objectives as well.

Quality as an integral part of project strategy

Previously in this chapter the importance of including quality in the earliest activities and preparation of any project has been discussed. The last of these major preparatory processes is the formulation of a strategy as to how the project objectives will satisfy the customer's needs (quality). Any objective that has not been met to the satisfaction of the customer is still incomplete.

Kimmons (1990) explains what a strategy is from a project point of view, namely: 'Strategy is that *system of logic* which will give the highest probability of achieving the defined project objectives while overcoming the identified problems.' The ultimate destination is the reaching of the project objectives, in an acceptable manner to the project, customer and, where necessary, the project stakeholders, with an acceptable intervention to the environment. Kimmons (1990) also indicates that the times of arrival, the overall cost of the journey and the direction and mode of travel all play a role in the successful achievement of the project objectives. It is important to be able to examine progressively as well as ultimately that both the intermediate and the ultimate objectives have been fully reached. This means that the project as a vehicle takes us to the destination, and does not stop or break down short of where it was intended to arrive.

The determination of this strategy must, in essence, be completed before conventional planning can commence. The planning process follows the approach formulated by the strategy and implements the strategy, with regards to reaching the specific destination, via a particular route, by means of a 'certain vehicle at an attainable speed of travel'.

If the achievement of the quality requirements is not included in this strategy then it is highly unlikely that it will be incorporated into the subsequent planning activities. It is during this strategic thinking phase that the project manager and his management team's knowledge, experience, skills and style will play the most important role. It is also during this stage that the mental 'die' of the project is 'cast'. This time is a combination of drawing on the resources of proven experience and the benchmarks it gives, together with lateral and original thinking, in order to produce the optimum solutions to specific project problems.

The fundamental issues affecting quality and its achievement, especially with regard to special objectives and problem areas, must be fully addressed during this phase, otherwise they will be left out of the rest of the project. Experience has shown that projects that have received careful and detailed effort in formulating of the appropriate strategies are far more successful than those where this aspect is glossed over, and where the management team remains within the confines of conventional approaches in order to try and solve unconventional problems.

It is during these early preparation and planning phases that a project management team truly earns their keep. Once this preparation and subsequent planning have been thoroughly worked through, the project manager's job is one of 'working the plan' and controlling the smooth running of the project, with the occasional course corrections and corrective action.

The development of the strategy must take the available resources into account. This will also include the ability of these resources to achieve the objectives successfully as well as demonstrate that they have been met. Strengths and weaknesses need to be analysed and the strengths capitalized upon in the project strategy, while the weaknesses need to be compensated for and worked around. In cases where areas of uncertainty exist, alternative scenarios must be developed for each case. Not only time and resources, but also quality must be correctly included in the strategy for addressing each scenario.

It is the well-thought-through project strategy that will devise ways to do things better for the specific project, as well as improve upon previous similar projects or similar parts of the project. Kimmons (1990) also includes in this strategic thinking process other items that are influenced further down the project process and which the author feels will influence quality, such as:

- sequencing of operations on the job site (which affects it);

- pattern of engineering, or other long lead time item's procurement;

- availability of skilled labour at the job site.

The author would like to add the following:

- 'constructability' or 'executability' of the design;

- project logic and priorities;

- execution plans;

- performance assurance (and measurement) plans;

- key areas in work breakdown structure;

- bey areas in project organization;

- basis for design and key project criteria.

The strategy must also address the project specific problems that were identified earlier, so that the risk of failing to overcome these is reduced to an acceptable minimum.

After the strategic thinking has been completed and documented to form the basis of the project policies, these must be thoroughly communicated to the whole project staff so that a unity of focus can be achieved in order to reach the project objectives. This strategic thinking process, while it needs to be led by the project manager, must be a team approach in order to eliminate the opportunities for omission and error. This is also necessary in order to achieve 'buy in' on the strategy by all concerned, especially the management and planning staff. It is only after all these strategic thinking and planning processes have been completed that the conventional project planning can occur.

Programme planning hierarchy

Programme planning is a demanding task which can become very detailed and complex, especially when the various inter-relationships are taken into account. It is for this reason that a hierarchy of task structuring (or work-breakdown) is necessary in order to help with the process of conceptualization. Generally the hierarchy is as follows:

- Project scope or statement of work to be performed.

- Project deliverables that comply with and add up to the scope (the deliverables must be quantified in terms of requirements, specifications and work breakdown structure) (WBS).

- Schedule of milestones of specific accomplishments.

In each of these elements that comprise the hierarchy, there are specific requirements and specifications that describe the level of success required in order for them to be of full value to the project and to contribute to the project success. The intermediate project customer, as well as the ultimate customer, pays for results and is only satisfied by the results that meet the given need.

All of these elements collectively form the total success, partial success or failure of the project. Therefore, how well each of these is achieved and satisfies the intermediate customer (the next activity that must use its outputs or results) has a direct bearing on the ultimate success, i.e. quality, together with cost and timeous completion, and goes to form the major determining factors of that success.

All work is a process, and for the work of planning to be a success (or a quality service) the process of planning a function must be approached in an orderly and systematic manner, to be sure that the opportunity for error is reduced to an absolute or acceptable minimum depending upon the importance of the issue.

Each of the activities in this hierarchy has a series of inputs and a conversion process in order to give the outputs, which form the input components of the next level in the hierarchy of activities. This next step could, among others, be the scheduling process or the process of determining the resources, services and materials/equipment required.

It is also important to establish and ensure that all the aspects affecting this process are credible and under control. Control measures to establish and demonstrate this must therefore also be developed and implemented. For example, if the project scope is incomplete or inaccurate, then the deliverables and requirements will also be incomplete or incorrect and so on, right down to the milestones of the project. This principle is applicable to the inputs, the process and its controlling factors, as well as to its outputs. Should errors or problems arise, they can be detected while (or very soon after) they happen and can be corrected before the incorrect information, schedule or document goes further and causes more 'knock-on' or ripple errors. This feedback loop, after assessment (or measurement) of acceptability, also allows for continuous, gradual improvement to information, systems, skills, experience and judgement.

This forms the basis of quality in planning. It is only possible through the use of competent planning personnel, systems, reliable and credible input and output information, and conversion systems to process this information.

The first two, namely people and systems, are often easier to verify from experience and track records than the third. The best method of assessing the reliability and credibility of input and output information is by referring back to proven case studies and benchmarking (similar successful and known best practice) projects. It is only when this hierarchy is worked back and summed up from the successful milestones (which flow from the WBS and lead to the deliverables, which must jointly satisfy the project scope) that a totally successful project can be accomplished.

These milestones must not only be specified (and accepted and paid for) in terms of time and cost, but also in terms of the quality of the facility or service accomplished. Of all the items in the hierarchy the WBS is probably the most important, because it breaks the project down into manageable work sections that can be conceptualized and managed successfully. It also becomes the 'project common denominator' for most other activities such as costing, scheduling quality plans, and lists of resources or 'bills of quantities'.

The WBS also facilitates the creation of networks that establish the project inter-relationships in terms of cost, time and completion critical activities, as well as quality of acceptable deliverables (for example, steelwork cannot be bolted onto concrete that has not set sufficiently, etc.). The size of the 'broken-down' work packages should be small enough to allow the work process of each work package, as well as the process inputs, controlling factors and outputs, to be able to be easily understood, defined and specified.

Quality and project planning

Quality and the planning process

The result or output of the project planning process is a clear, namely an all embracing operational plan which initiates, regulates and guides the whole project from the output of the strategic planning activities to the final completion and handover to the customer.

This plan must take the four result areas or project components into account and ensure that they are properly interfaced into a single approach. These components are the project scope, the project deliverables and their success measurements, the budget and available resources, and the schedule and time constraints. It is necessary to break the total task that is to be accomplished into manageable and measurable units of work, starting with the work breakdown structure (WBS).

Oberlender (1993) lists the key principles for planning and scheduling in Figure 3.1, namely:

- Begin planning before starting work, rather than after starting work.

- Involve people who will actually do the work in the planning and scheduling process.

- Include all aspects of the project: scope, budget, schedule and quality.

- Build flexibility into the plan, and include allowance for changes and time for review and approvals.

- Remember the schedule is the plan for doing the work and it will never be precisely correct.

- Keep the plan simple, eliminate irrelevant details that prevent the plan from being readable. (Irrelevant detail includes using vocabulary that may be strange to the persons executing the plan.)

- Communicate the plan to all parties; any plan is worthless unless it is known.

Kerzner (1989) states that 'total programme planning cannot be accomplished unless all of the necessary information becomes available at project initiation'. These information requirements are:

- the statement of work (SOW);

- the project specifications;

- the work breakdown structure (WBS);

- the milestone schedule.

The author would like to link success measurement factors (achievement of quality) to both the project specification and the 'milestone schedule'. This is necessary in order to be able to progressively, as well as finally demonstrate to the customer that what they required and ordered has been met. The activities of measuring and demonstrating success consume time and resources and if allowance is not made for these in the project plan then they are often omitted, or at best only given superficial attention, because of time and budget constraints.

Management criteria for project planning inputs

Project Specification
    Project scope:

- criteria for acceptance by customer;

- time limitations;

- budget limitations;

- resource limitations;

FIGURE 3.1 Process of project preplanning and preparation

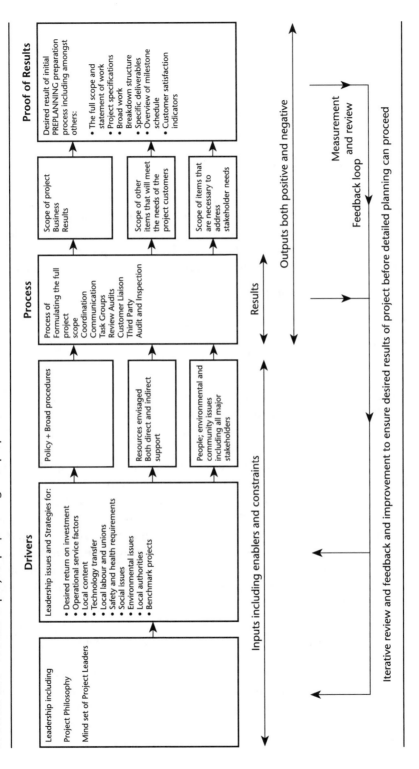

- process design;

- yechnology available;

- personnel required;

- special 'site' requirements;

- health and safety requirements;

- environmental requirements;

- legal or statutory requirements.

The work breakdown structure provides the common framework for interrelated activities. Large or complex projects are often broken down into 'sub-projects' which can be regarded as discrete projects in their own right. The major levels of a work breakdown structure are the following:

- project or 'sub-project';

- task;

- sub-task;

- work packages.

The greater levels of detail are listed as the sub-tasks, and work packages are developed from these. This allows for effective use of work flow diagrams like PERT. The appropriate quality activities and success indicators for each of these must be included.

It is usual that at the sub-task and work package level quality plans are developed. It is advisable to involve the customer in the drafting of these tasks and packages even if it is only on a review and acceptance level so that 'buy in' by the customer is ensured and the opportunity for conflict is reduced. A customer who feels comfortable with the project as it progresses is one who accepts the quality of the milestones and the final result more readily. This process starts at the earliest stages of the project. The summation of the work packages into a sub-task, the sub-tasks into a task and the tasks into a project must ultimately result in the accomplishment of the whole project scope.

The WBS should follow and meet the specified requirements of the project. The WBS is designed and developed by the planning office, but the work is carried out by other people who must also accept that the tasks and work packages are achievable and realistic. It is also necessary to develop and specify the success measurement factors for each of these so that those who perform the work will know how and to what standard they will be measured, during the performance of a task and after the achievement of a milestone. This will also determine when a (part) payment can be made for the successful completion and acceptable quality of the milestone.

The contract must be structured in such a manner that payment is only made after successful accomplishment of a milestone has been demonstrated. This principle reinforces the discipline that payment is only made for successful (quality) work. The work breakdown structure should itself be regarded as a discrete deliverable and must be subjected to progressive review and approval by a competent third party team to ensure completeness and acceptability.

Kerzner (1989) states that the WBS provides a basis for:

- the responsibility matrix;

- network scheduling;

- costing;

- risk analysis.

The constant use of quality principles, techniques and procedures in each of the elements becomes the integrating factor to ensure success.

Work planning and authorization

The final authorization as part of the quality process

The authorization to commence with work as well as the task to be accomplished is based on the project plan. This authorization is usually linked to funds and schedule as well as interrelated tasks. These authorizations are formal and link to the project contract, which will ultimately allow for payment at the completion of the task.

The process of authorization to proceed with a task or job should also be formally closed off with the authorization that the quality related requirements have been fully met, and that the success determinants of the tasks as set out in the approved project plan have also been fully complied with. This authorization should be the ultimate approval for payment to be made for the completion of the task.

Allow for the 'people' part of quality

The approval to continue with a task also implies that suitable labour and man hours will be recruited and deployed. It is important to plan orientation and special skills training time into this phase of the planning activity. The success and standard of any project is heavily dependent upon the level of motivation, experience and skills of the people deployed. The planned number of hours to complete a task must be achievable but tight. This builds in a stretch element which constantly reinforces a sense of urgency.

If insufficient time is allowed the work will be rushed, short cuts will be taken and quality will be compromised. The negative cost and schedule implications of allowing too much time are axiomatic. It is advisable to establish a benchmark from similar projects or applicable parts of successful projects that have been completed as a standard. This standard is not only applicable to man hours but also to the planning, specification and achievement of acceptable levels of quality.

Include quality in materials and procurement planning

The authorization to commence with work will usually lead to the formulation of a procurement plan. This plan must allow for the review of specifications and contracts prior to orders being placed on a supplier.

If the specifications are incorrect or incomplete then there is little chance that the correct product, be it material, equipment or a service, will be procured. Time must be allowed for an independent review of these documents prior to procurement negotiations to ensure the correct level of quality. This is usually performed by the quality department in conjunction with personnel with the appropriate technical skills.

When an order is about to be placed, the requisition also needs to be reviewed for correctness to ensure that what was negotiated and agreed to is included in the requisition. This action also absorbs time and needs to be included in the plan. It is important for a third party to review the order prior to placing it to ensure clarity and accuracy of information.

It is advisable to include somebody from the quality department in the procurement negotiating team to ensure that quality is negotiated into the transaction from the beginning and not left out of the transaction. If quality, especially special progress inspections, tests and documentation demonstrating the successful completion of a task or contract, is not negotiated into the contract from the very beginning there is little chance of receiving the desired level of quality after a contract is signed.

Many organizations adopt an approach that if you want quality and documentation 'it will cost you'. Experience has taught that organizations which adopt that attitude do not fully understand quality and have not embraced the ethical and value adding as well as the waste saving possibilities of the quality approach, which will make their product more competitive, not more expensive. Avoid doing business with these organizations because they will cost the project more money and time in the long run due to the difficulties that will be experienced in bringing their products up to standard, or even having to re-order from another supplier at a late stage of the project.

Quality and project planning inputs and products

The project plan should include all the major decisions and events of the project. The planning team will take decisions based on the project strategy as discussed previously as well as other input information. The quality of this information, i.e. its accuracy and relevance, also need to be examined before they are used, otherwise 'garbage in will be garbage out'.

The product of the planning process also needs to be reviewed by a suitably experienced and qualified third party to ensure relevance and applicability. The output of this activity is the decision as to who will do what, how, when, for how long, with what resources and what are the success measurement factors.

William E Smith in Chapter 1 of Section V of *Project Management: A Reference for Professionals* gives lists for the following:

- information required for planning;

- components of the plan;

- details of planning.

These are reproduced here by kind permission of the publishers Marcel Dekker Inc. in Tables 3.1, 3.2, 3.3.

The author has added next to each of the items on the list some of the typical quality aspects of the item that will have to be taken into account. These are generic and serve as memory joggers, and the specific quality requirements for each project will have to be determined for each activity or output.

Table 3.3. is an expansion of these items, and the typical quality items are listed next to each aspect. These aspects can vary from project to project but will serve as a valuable first step in the project 'customization' process for each of these steps. This table serves as an introduction to the matrix of the last part of this book.

TABLE 3.1 Information required for planning

Type of Information	Quality Aspects
1. The type of project, its capacity and location	– Market & customer needs and requirements of the product or service.
	– Product or service specifications and market predictions of specification trends and improvements needed.
	– Environmental and demographic requirements of the stakeholders.
2. The scope of work to be performed	– Include the reference to all the specifications for each item of the scope.
	– List the acceptability criteria or success measurement factors for the items on the scope.
3. A preliminary cost estimate	– Include the cost of the various quality related tasks.
	– Lump as little as possible together as overheads.
	– Include the estimate of the cost of quality.
4. The site variation report	– All quality matters affecting variations.
5. A preliminary schedule of major milestones or objectives	– The requirements and specifications of each milestone need to be listed.
	– The method of or procedure for measuring the successful completion must be listed.
6. Pertinent contract requirements	– Include all specific quality requirements of the products, facilities and service, both interim and final for equipment, system requirements and specifications.
7. Special design and/or construction requirements	– Success and acceptance test and methods.
8. Climate restrictions	– Verification of correctness of information.
	– Have climatic extremes been correctly identified and quantified?

TABLE 3.1 *Continued*

Type of Information	Quality Aspects
9. Environmental studies, feasibility reports etc.	– Acceptability to relevant authorities and environmental groups.
	– Review of strengths and weaknesses analysis.
	– Acceptability to potential stakeholders.
10. Proposal documents	– List quality aspects and requirements in the proposal.
	– List quality and other aspects of the proposal that will require special attention.

Source: Reproduced with kind permission of the publishers Marcel Dekker Inc. and based on tables of Section V in Chapter 1 by William E Smith *of Project Management: A Reference for Professionals* (1989) edited by Kimmons, Robert L and Lowrence, James H.

TABLE 3.2 Items that should be included in any project plan

1. Division of responsibilities between the owner, contractor, and any third parties involved in the project

2. The engineering plan

3. The procurement plan

4. Logistics planning (information material services control)

5. The quality control plan

6. The construction plan

7. The financial plan

8. The commissioning and start up plan.

The quality control plan also contains the information that integrates reviews and reports on the broad quality activities of the project. The other items in this table each have relevant quality aspects of their own which determine the success of the activity. These are directly related to the activity and are usually activity specific.

Source: Reproduced with kind permission of the publishers Marcel Dekker Inc. and based on tables of Section V in Chapter 1 by William E Smith of *Project Management: A Reference for Professionals* (1989) edited by Kimmons, Robert L and Lowrence, James H.

TABLE 3.3 Some details of planning and the related quality aspects
(this is not intended to be a comprehensive list but to give an indication of
typical quality aspects.)

Planning item	Typical quality aspects
Construction and Planning	
1. Facility realization sequence	Critical aspects of the sequence and specifications to be determined and highlighted.
2. Temporary facilities, offices, warehousing etc.	Special climatic or other requirements for work to be performed in them, or items to be stored in them.
3. Tool and equipment requirements	List special capabilities, accuracy repeatability and other measurement calibration and safety requirements.
4. Labour availability and productivity	Special skills, unusual working hours and conditions as well as performance testing and specific qualifications.
5. Camp requirements	Special requirements of utilities, climatic conditions, access and environmental considerations.
6. Work week and productivity impact	List tasks that will require unusual working hours such as night time X- or gamma ray examination, and establish measurements to measure re-work and scrap.
7. Climatic effects on field work	Training and awareness to cope with, for example, extreme heat or cold, diseases, dehydration as well as the effect of climate on equipment, materials, processes and their behaviour.
8. Field engineering assistance required	Clearly list and include in the contract the deliverables, requirements and specifications of field engineering.
9. Extent of sub-contracting	List special quality training or orientation that sub-contractors will require.
10. Field organization and staffing	Include all quality related staff as well as deployment dates.

TABLE 3.3 *Continued*

Planning item	Typical quality aspects
Procurement planning	
1. Procurement sources (equipment materials and information)	Quality ratings, such as ISO 9001 status, audit reports of suppliers of equipment and materials.
2. Home office as well as field procurement	Drafting of procurement procedures including quality aspects for both.
3. Long lead time items	Special progressive quality assurance checks as well as final inspection and testing to ensure timeous detection and correction of errors.
4. Expediting	Policies and procedures for expediting which will not compromise quality requirements.
5. Logistical planning	List quality aspects that affect each major quality related item or contract and allow time and resources for these to be achieved. Include quality aspects from the earliest negotiations through contract execution to payment and closeout.
Planning items for engineering planning	
1. Sources of technology and information	Review of applicability of source with special emphasis on limitations and strengths.
2. Code specifications and standards to be used	Review correctness of code chosen relevant to statutory, contractual or design safety and environmental requirements.
3. Utilization of counselling	Report on 'curriculum vitae' as well as applicability of experience relative to task and cost – value adding ability of the consultant.
4. Early work	List and contract for the deliverables, the requirements and specifications intended.

TABLE 3.3   *Continued*

Planning item	*Typical quality aspects*
5. Requisitioning priorities	Include quality aspects in this list especially where quality will lead to increased lead time or special documentation requirements.
6. Drawing priorities	Review whether all quality requirements of the drawings are clearly listed in the correct sequence and prioritized.
7. Vendor data requirements	Vendor rating which includes quality as well as ISO 9001 listing status.
8. Utilization of scale models	List special quality requirements or objectives of the scale model.
9. Manpower requirements	Include quality related staff as well as special quality training or orientation qualifications, along with special skills of the rest of the manpower to be established and specified.
10. Approval requirements	These to include both formal and informal special quality related reviews and acceptance steps.
11. Organization and staffing	Organization to include success and progressive quality review reporting mechanics.
12. Utilization of prefabricated modules	Include quality requirements in the contract as well as type of inspection and testing at the pre-fabricators' premises. Include specific quality documentation manuals as part of the final acceptance procedures prior to payment.

Planning items for quality control planning

1. Audit of design of equipment systems services for conformance to specifications	The auditors to be competent in the particular technological field. The quality auditors need to be thoroughly trained and qualified in quality auditing techniques. Audits to be performed in accordance with an approved procedure.

TABLE 3.3 *Continued*

Planning item	*Typical quality aspects*
2. Checking of calculations and drawings	To be performed by competent third party design engineers and draft persons working to approved procedures.
3. Shop inspection of equipment and fabricated items	The activity to be specified in the contract. Inspection stages and details to be specified by the design engineer together with chief inspector. Drawings and specifications to be current and where necessary procedures to be specified.
4. Certification of materials	Lot or batch size and sampling procedures to be specified. Statistical methods where applicable to be called up. Only competent laboratories and personnel to be used for tests.
5. Certification of welding procedures	Procedure type and determination to be compatible with relevant code of fabrication. Thorough list of formally approved procedures and welders to be kept.
6. Receiving and inspection of equipment and material	An approved receipt inspection procedure to exist. Special receipt inspection specifications per item where applicable to be used.
7. Job site storage and environmental protection of equipment and materials	Manufacturers and/or designers to specify their requirements in a special document. This must also include preservation after installation while waiting for commissioning, including special lubricants, rotation of equipment, protection of exposed seal faces, etc.
8. Construction inspection	List of areas where construction inspection is to be carried out and by whom with what skills. List areas where quality plans are required and what documentation should be generated. Specify acceptance criteria for final as well as interim inspection activities.

TABLE 3.3 *Continued*

Planning item	Typical quality aspects
Logistics planning – typical items	
Shipping limitations	Specify special packaging or restraining requirements in order to preserve the quality of the final product. Times of shipping because of a specific 'weather window' to perform the task.
Poor or limiting facilities	Facilities may have to be upgraded, or temporary facilities hired in order to be able to perform tasks to the specified standard.
Customers' special requirements	This usually does not present a problem if properly identified and planned for up front, unless there are long delays which can lead to deterioration of product quality.
Inland transport	Where transportation infrastructure is poor, special anti-variation, weather resting and/or handling crates or packaging may need to be specified.
Weather restraints	Allowance must be made in the design and packaging for extreme heat, cold, humidity, dryness or corrosive conditions. For example, correct selection of materials for extreme cold, special heat sinks for electronics working in extreme heat or de-humidification for damp conditions, etc.
Financial planning	
1. Cash flow requirements	Allow for the costs of quality activities.
2. Progress payments and billing frequency	Only pay against milestones which have met acceptable quality standards and have all the required documentation complete.
3. Impact of financial sources (financiers)	The financier must not only be pre-occupied by cost and schedule results, but must also take quality requirements into account in order to assure the long-term viability of the investment.

TABLE 3.3 *Continued*

Planning item	Typical quality aspects
Commissioning plan	
1. Pre-operational checkout	All documentation approving or accepting all deliverables in accordance with specifications and tests to be available before the activity is commenced.
2. Commissioning operations	Plans for commissioning and operations to include all the quality steps and activities as well as procedures prior to commencement.
3. Initial operations	All important procedures to be in place beforehand, as well as specifications of results.
4. Performance testing	Specified test results, procedures and instrument calibration to be available in advance.
Job closeout	
1. 'As built' drawings	To be reviewed for correctness and user friendliness. To be stored safely and in a retrievable manner.
2. Manuals and records required by the client	Maintenance and/or operations to accept these before closeout. The quality department to review and accept all relevant records before closeout. Link the acceptance of these to the final closeout payment or payment of retention money.
3. Record retention	Record retention policy, procedures and facilities to be in place and successfully assessed before final closeout.
4. Final job report	To be complete and include a section on quality.
5. Release of retention monies	This can only be performed after all quality aspects are acceptable to operations and maintenance of the customer.

Reproduced with kind permission of the publishers Marcel Dekker Inc. and based on tables of Section V in Chapter 1 by William E Smith of *Project Management: A Reference for Professionals* (1989) edited by Kimmons, Robert L and Lowrence, James H.

The influence of schedule on quality

The project activity schedule is one of the key items that can affect quality on a project after the planning has been successfully completed and the various quality related aspects included. This is because quality is always the result of careful thought, planning and effort. If insufficient time is allowed to complete a task properly or to perform the various quality related activities, then short cuts are taken. Kerzner (1989) states that scheduling is the next major activity after the go-ahead has been given to the programme and project plan. The project manager has to schedule work from the very beginning, even before the planning has commenced, if all the preparatory items are to be dealt with in time.

Kimmons (1990) points out that 'it is necessary to draft an early work schedule in which all the initial activities, assigned responsibilities and completion dates are established and listed'. This early work schedule must of necessity include the various quality and quality related activities so that they are included in the initial work. Omissions at this stage will have a ripple effect of omissions throughout the project. These items have already been discussed in the preceding parts of this chapter and need to be included in the early work schedule.

The schedule should preferably be designed in such a manner that it can be used as both an internal management document as well as a communication document to the customer and stakeholders.

The project schedule is one of the key facts which determines the deployment of resources, the interface between activities and schedules, and consequently the project synergy. Project synergy is vital if quality is to be achieved. However, inversely, the requirements for the success of the project deliverables (quality) will also help drive the project's synergy. Kerzner (1989) points out that 'the activity schedule is invaluable for projecting time-phased resource utilization requirements as well as providing a basis for visually tracking performance'.

The measurement of success, which is one of the functions of quality (not necessarily the Quality Group) and the successful meeting of requirements and achieving of milestones, flows directly out of the activity schedule. Success measurement should also be scheduled as a discrete and important activity in its own right. This measurement and reporting against the standard, (namely the project plan and schedule) and the taking of corrective action becomes one of project management's significant tasks during the project execution phase. In other words, the schedule helps drive quality as one of the four major management result areas of a project. The other three are quantity, i.e. assessing the correct number of deliverables at acceptable specification levels at the required milestones, and keeping the project on time and within budget.

Kerzner (1989) gives certain guidelines that should be followed during the preparation of schedules. The author would like to include some quality related expansions to these, as the achievement of quality is also an item to be included in the schedule. These are:

- *All major events and dates must be clearly identified.* A major event has only been fully described when its specifications and types of tests for successful achievement have also been included.

- *The exact sequence of work should be defined through a network in which interrelationships between events can be identified.* The assessment and reporting of the successful completion is an event in its own right and must be included. In many instances the quality aspects such as tests and evaluations form an integral part of the sequence of work and must be clearly highlighted and included in the schedule. An example of this is the inspection and radiographic approval of the root run of a critical weld; this can only be carried out immediately after the completion of the root run. The inspection and acceptance of this root run must visibly be included in the schedule. The approval of the placement and acceptability of concrete re-informing prior to the pouring of concrete is another example.

- *Schedules should relate directly to the Work Breakdown Structure.* This requires that the schedule clearly indicates where a task starts and finishes. A task starts with an acceptable work force as well as information, equipment, tools and materials. These inputs all have a quality implication which the performer of the task must be aware of and must be scheduled to verify. The same is applicable to the completion of a task, namely that the performer of the task must be the first person to be able to verify or take part in the verification process that the task has been successfully completed.

- *All schedules must identify the time constraints and, if possible, should identify those resources required for each event.* Time must be allowed to perform the various quality related activities, whether they are performed by the person carrying out the task, by the in-house quality groups or even by a third party.

In instances where the schedule – because of a combination of circumstances – compromises quality, this should be immediately negotiated with the customer (internal or external) so that an alternative arrangement can be made.

The schedule should also be subjected to the principles of quality assurance. The vital role that the schedule plays means that it should be subjected to progressive, as well as a final formal review by a third party who is a competent planner and scheduler. This is necessary to ensure that no items have been missed, and that the correct amount of time and any other resources have also been allocated. This review will also have to establish whether the correct responsibilities and interfaces have been set up so that the necessary project synergy will be achieved.

One of the major synergy building aspects of a schedule and its related activities is an ability to pinpoint possible clashes of interest and the resultant conflict. The author's experience has taught that where there is a clash because of a conflict of interest, quality as the softest project deliverable and management result area will almost always be compromised.

Kimmons (1990) lists the sequence in which the various scheduling activities should be done as follows:

- task identification;

- sequencing;

- logic diagram;

- staffing analysis;

- activity duration;

- the critical path;

- resource profile;

- resource levelling;

- schedule plan;

- bar charts.

Each of these activities has a dual quality component, namely their involvement of the quality steps needed to achieve and demonstrate success of the deliverables, as well as the independent competent review correction/improvement and acceptance of the schedule activity as a project management deliverable in its own right.

Quality and fast tracking

Fast tracking is a method that is frequently used when projects have limited time available for completion. Williams (1995) defines a fast track project as 'those that are completed in less than 70 per cent of the time it takes to do "traditional" projects'.

Traditionally with fast track projects the same or a similar amount of work has to be done in less time, usually at the expense of optimal preparation. Very often they took just as long because of the high amount of corrective action needed due to the errors resulting from the rush. Fast tracking often had a very negative effect on the ultimate project quality, and cognizance of this fact had to be taken when the decision to use the fast track approach was taken. This is often because the networked, intermediate review steps were minimized and often even eliminated.

The use of the fast track approach is now becoming more popular as international competition increases and new products or services have to reach the market before those of the opposition. Projects of shorter duration need not cost more, and there are many instances where the time saved has lowered labour costs and enabled a facility to be economically productive, leading to overall financial benefits to the customer. The steadily increasing cost of labour has led to the scenario on many projects where the cost of labour is greater than the cost of materials, and it is more cost effective to reduce labour costs at the expense of optional material utilization.

Fast track projects require a whole paradigm shift as far as project management planning and scheduling are concerned. The project team needs to become more multi-functional, trusting and supportive without the fear of finger pointing and blame allotment. Williams (1995) states: 'The old ideas of control and suspicion and minimizing risks are giving way to the new ones of trust, empowerment, openness, customer focus, and taking smart risks.' These are the values that are also espoused by modern quality management. It will require a paradigm shift on behalf of the (quality) management team and their approach to managing for quality on projects.

The whole system of repeated reviews and very comprehensive 'paper trails' will have to be reviewed. This will require that the fast track design-build team will have to include a quality professional from the very beginning, and that only the most necessary review and documentation actions must be included in this process. In many areas some of the documentation for self-protecting reasons will have to be replaced by trust.

It is important to note that facility and product quality as well as bodily risk or health cannot be compromised at any stage of the fast track project. The need to 'freeze' the design at an earlier stage of the project will often resolve in a facility that is not as versatile as would have been possible. Williams (1995) also states: 'Fast track projects do not strive for better communications and trust. They require it'.

A very thorough and sound project and construction schedule into which all the important elements have been built (including quality) is a prerequisite for a successful fast track project. This requires that the pre-emptive and preventive actions to avoid errors which are one of the cornerstones of quality are vital. The whole team must anticipate eventualities and plan for the prevention of these opportunities for error well in advance. The money and effort put into this stage, when things are relatively calm and large amounts of resources and capital have not yet been committed, can often be saved many times over when the pressure and rush of the project is on.

It is important to bring the suppliers on board as early as possible and include them in the project team. This is an extension of the manufacturing quality principle of regarding the external supplier as part of the manufacturing team. The early involvement of suppliers improves communication and commitment to the project. It also enables the design-build team to avoid specifying items or processes that are time consuming, difficult, or costly for the supplier to realize.

The traditional quality system of the procurement process will have to be re-designed to use only the vital checks for product quality and safety. Trusting the selection of the correct supplier with the correct capabilities is vital. Checking and re-checking of documentation can be avoided if the supplier is on board, involved from the design stage and is committed to the success of the project. The principle of limited re-work must be accepted from the beginning, and when it does happen it must not be accompanied by finger pointing and blame allotment. On a fast track project the maximization of wealth or value creation can require limited amounts of re-work to achieve.

Project plans and schedules in fast track projects should be subjected to an even more careful scrutiny because the fast tracking approach almost always has the potential for a clash of interest which compromises quality in one way or another.

Successful Fast track projects will usually have the following features:

- meticulously planning;

- require many more resources for a set time;

- must be regularly reviewed at shorter intervals;

- make use of increased high level supervision and skilled workers;

- require extremely close co-operation, attention and co-ordination (three difficult tasks to co-ordinate at the same time);

- the basic quality criteria are never compromised;

- strong clear leadership;

- every team member must accept the reasons for fast tracking;

- use only experienced personnel with proven track records, because little time is available for training and learning drives;

- involve the suppliers at the design stage;

- team trust and support must be very strong and replace blame and finger pointing.

The unit times that can be used for the fast track activity are often published, and these can be used as a form of quality control on the time related inputs. These published norms should be reviewed even more carefully when greenfield projects, special labour or skills problems etc. can exist or arise.

It is important to realize that a schedule is project specific and therefore of limited time duration, but that poor quality of plant or facility can impact on the long-term future life, safety, reliability or profitability of the facility which the project was established to create. Therefore, the customer must be careful that the important project factor of time (schedule or the lack of sufficient time) does not overrule quality, or lead to undesirable quality short cuts which usually compromise doing the job properly the first time.

CASE STUDY: APOLLO 13

The well documented Apollo 13 lunar project is an example of how a fast track project can be thrust on a project management team.

The loss of one of the major oxygen tanks and other equipment due to the rupture immediately changed the project objective from one of landing the astronauts on the moon to one of aborting the lunar landing and bringing them all back alive using the resources available. The whole new project had to be rescheduled in hours not months, and consisted of many sub-projects all on a fast track.

Several messages about this project were clearly made very early in the project, namely:

- Very strong project leadership was given.

- The success of any fast track project is heavily dependent on the project directorship's leadership and style.

- Strong clear dedicated leadership of a competent team that respects the leadership, but that is free to contribute and whose contribution is respected, is essential if a fast track project is to succeed.

- The leadership and supervision of the project directorship was always available and rigorous reviews were conducted at short intervals to ensure continuity and maintenance of focus.

- The objective of the project was clear in the minds of every person working on the project, namely to bring the entire crew back alive.

- Every team member was dedicated and focused on the task at hand, and no private agendas or actions that could diffuse the focus and effort of the team were allowed.

- The team functioned very effectively and there was a high level of trust between members.

- The whole team was prepared to go the extra mile (or ten in this case) in order to ensure that every milestone was successfully achieved in its correct sequence.

- The people and skills employed were of a very high calibre and they were allowed the room to think laterally in order to arrive at a solution to the problem. All solutions were tested for success and 'procedurized' in spite of the extremely difficult time constraints.

- The astronauts were the primary customer and their basic needs were well defined and monitored. From time to time specific needs were negotiated.

- In instances where the customer's needs were compromised, the situation was discussed with the customer and their buy-in and input obtained.

- The deliverables and their success parameters were clearly formulated and accepted up front by everybody. (An example of this is the lack of availability of energy for the re-entry procedure. The available energy was calculated and a modified re-entry procedure had to be formulated and tested to meet these requirements in time for the re-entering of the craft into the earth's atmosphere.)

- The principles of quality were never compromised, with every new action being tested at command control and a procedure formulated before being transmitted to the space craft for use.

The success of this project is born out by the fact that all the astronauts were brought home safely. This can be regarded as an extreme case-study, but because it is well documented, even to the extent of being on video, it can be easily studied and the correct principles of fast tracking that were applied can be observed.

Some management–customer communication techniques

Planning involves the effective use of resources and ways in which they can best be managed and controlled. It is important to keep the customers up to date with these methods and their results so that they still feel satisfied that the project is under control, i.e. that the quality of deliverables will be acceptable, and within the budget and time frame.

Authorization of the WBS by both the project manager and the customer is important. This activity must be expanded to include authorization of schedules and key resources at key stages, so that both management and the customer are assured that the project is under control and on track. This will also include the acceptance and communication of summary networks which show the inter-relationship of tasks and their deliverables, and what their earliest and latest start and finish times are. These progress measurements against the standard can be reflected and communicated to the customer as part of the progress report.

It is important to stress that no task is completed until it has been proven to be acceptable (inspection, testing, commissioning, etc.) and the relevant documentation, recording and attesting to this fact is completed.

The communication of the successful completion of these quality activities is extremely important to the customer and to keeping them in their 'comfort zone'. Customer satisfaction on a project (or other tasks) is dependent on open factual and credible communication of the project's progress against the consumption of available resources and time.

It is equally important to reassure the customer that their resources are being effectively utilized by not only reporting on the desired achievement of the milestones, but by demonstrating the acceptability of the completed milestones. Many customers will insist that they have a shadow team of their own stationed on the project. This creates a very fast and credible feedback loop, but does not relieve the project management team from the duty of clear, concise and user friendly reporting of the project's progress. It is advisable to place the senior members of the customer's operations and maintenance staff in such a team because this can also serve as a training activity. These people will keep a watchful eye on progress because they will inherit the shortcomings of the project and have to live with them for a long time. This approach serves as a valuable quality control review and information gathering mechanism for the customer.

The customer's own quality team will also need to be involved from the very beginning in order to ascertain and report on the success of the integrated quality system and its execution separately. Open and clear reporting to the project stakeholders on a regular basis is becoming increasingly important, because stakeholder satisfaction is an element of quality in its own right. There are several examples where stakeholder outcry has involved the politicians and led to negative press reporting, resulting in a costly time-consuming rearguard action by the project management. This is especially true where the project can have a negative impact on the environment, people's health or socio-political side effects.

Some examples of such problems are:

- the oil exploration and extraction projects in Nigeria;

- the extraction of heavy metals out of the costal dunes in ecologically sensitive areas in South Africa;

- the dismantling of an oil platform in the North Sea.

Communication at higher levels must be supported by accurate measurement methods and factual data, and must convey management information on which decisions can be made. This is often done graphically. The following is a list of some of the common graphical methods.

- bar charts;

- milestone charts and diagrams;

- charts of performance comparison with the standard or plan;

- pie diagrams;

- logic flow diagrams;

- critical path networks;

- 'pert charts'.

It is also important to report the progress and achievement of success on the project as it happens. This can be in the form of specified results or performance versus actual results achieved in the project, test or inspection programmes.

In short, the reporting of the achievement of success against the various milestones and their requirements and specifications is an important quality aspect, and is the responsibility of project management in order to help reassure the customer and stakeholders that their interests are being served – or at least, not negated.

Quality plans

A very useful, and often essential, part of the management control (for quality) function, is the use of quality plans. They are normally used on special, complicated, or critical tasks, and are not drawn up for routine activities which are adequately covered by normal trade training and discipline.

In their simplest form, they are based on the breakdown of activities in the work packages. Each task is listed and against each task the following details needed for its success are also reflected. This gives confidence that each aspect of the work has been carried out successfully, i.e. the task description and its:

- deliverables;

- specifications;

- procedure or work instruction number that governs the performance of the task (where applicable);

- success measurement specification and methods;

- signature/s (of individuals, as well as foremen or inspectors, where necessary) confirming that the task has successfully been completed;

- any special instructions or requirements relating to the task;

- final acceptance that the work package as a whole has successfully been completed.

All the accepted quality plans, confirming that all the tasks for a specific milestone (or sub-project) were performed correctly, can be placed in a single total data package for ease of review and handover during commissioning. These packages give an 'audit trail' of successful work completed against approved design inputs and specifications in order to give a credible end result.

The process work model is applicable to quality plans as well, and time must be scheduled to allow for review and approval of the quality plans against the design requirements of the WBS, along with work packages both prior to and after completion of the task. This gives acceptable inputs, i.e. prior reviewed and approved quality plans and acceptable work process, namely working to the approved tasks, systems, procedures, work instructions and acceptable output requirements. The quality plan includes signatures attesting not only to successful work performed, but also to successful inspection and test of the desired end result, as well as the successful completion of corrective action.

The use of quality plans, therefore, completes the control loop for management and provides feedback that the plans that were formulated, reviewed and approved have ultimately been successfully carried out. The output can be the actual acceptance criteria for final takeover. A further advantage of quality plans is that they clearly indicate point responsibility and accountability for the successful performance of each work stage. They can also be drawn up for almost any task on a project. The following is an example of a typical quality plan.

QUALITY PLAN PROJECT NAME . . . . **DATE DRAFTED** . . . .

WORK BREAKDOWN AREA OR PACKAGE . . . . DATE EXECUTED . . . .

WORK PACKAGE / TASK IDENTIFICATION DESCRIPTION . . . . I D NO . . . .

SYSTEM IDENTIFICATION / LOCATION . . . .

INFORMATION NECESSARY FOR PERFORMING THE TASK SUCCESSFULLY

DESCRIPTION AND DIAGRAM NO: PROCEDURES & WORK INSTRUCTION: NO OF DOCUMENTS TO BE COMPLETED:

. . . .

. . . .

. . . .

ITEM: **DESCRIPTION OF:**   **PROCEDURE NO:**   **SPECIFICATION NO:**   **TEST RESULTS:**   **RESPONSIBILITY:**   **SIGNATURE:**

	SPEC	ACTUAL:	PERF:	INSP:	TEST:	APPROV:	COMMENT

SEQ NO: ACTIVITY include both the work execution and testing as separate activities:

REWORK ACTIVITIES

RESPONSIBILITY LEGEND: **OP** – Perform task   **IS** – Inspect self   **FI** – Foreman Inspect   **IA** – Inspector approve

HP – Hold point   **WP** – Witness point by customers   **TT** – Test team   **CA** – Customer accept

FINAL ACCEPTANCE SIGN . . . .   **NAME (print)** . . . .   **SIGN OFF DATE** . . . .

CHAPTER FOUR

The application of quality management principles to development and design

Quality starts with concept and design

The principles of quality can also be applied to development and design and are a valuable management tool as projects grow out of development opportunities and facilities are designed to meet the market or customer need highlighted by these opportunities.

The role and importance of design is often not appreciated by management and as a result the opportunity for error and the compromising of the product or service quality at the design stage is unacceptably high. This can be illustrated by some of the statistics collected by the Design Council in Britain, namely:

- Only 27 per cent of companies have a corporate policy favourable to good design.

- Only 20 per cent of designers were adequately briefed.

- Only 10 per cent of design projects were subjected to a design brief.

- Only 6 per cent of companies had suitable policies for ensuring that their designers were kept up to date by appropriate training.

The results of the Design Council in Britain also showed that even with modern products, design could still be improved and re-design could achieve the following:

- 24 per cent reduction in manufacturing costs.

- 29 per cent improvement on market demand.

- 37 per cent improvement in capital tied up in stocks and 'work in progress'.

The principles and approach discussed will help to reduce the opportunity for error during development and design, thus minimizing the extremely high risk and cost that often accompany errors during development and design. The reader is however referred to the international codes and design handbooks for further information on design principles and practices, such as BS 7000 (1989) (R4.2) *Guide to Managing Product Design*.

This is a guide that emphasizes that design, like any activity, should be regarded as a process and be managed in a similar manner to any other activity in an organization or business. The guide outlines how product design should be managed, and the levels of excellence that a design division needs to achieve.

Quality in the development of products and systems in a pre-project phase

One of the explanations or definitions of the word 'development' would be *to bring from a latent or inactive state to an active, fuller state* (based on the definition of 'development' in the *Oxford English Dictionary*.)

The concept clearly implies that there is a change of state, not necessarily an addition of knowledge, although invariably this happens. During development the underlying principles and opportunities that have already been established or demonstrated (often during research) now have to be converted into usable products and services by means of a facility which the project must build or establish. The increase in sophistication of products and systems increases the need for careful, thorough and traceable development and, in practice, there are many statistics that illustrate this.

Experience has shown that in new chemical plants approximately 40 per cent of the money spent to correct, fix and re-work plants can be related to lack of proper product, system and process development, so that they are fit for purpose when designed, built, erected and installed into an integrated plant or system.

In electronic equipment, many field failures (in the order of 40–43 per cent) are due to engineering design and development inadequacies. This is due to the fact that it is not a straightforward task to take basic scientific and engineering principles and data and convert them into usable, robust products that are user friendly and problem free. These difficulties also extend to the facilities (or plant) for their manufacture or realization.

Generally, the statistics indicate (be it chemical, electrical, electronic, mechanical or similar industries) that approximately 40 per cent of the end use problems can be traced back to poor engineering and a lack of thorough, careful development. The irony of the matter is that, if it costs 'X' amount to correct a problem arising during the development phase, then it usually costs more than 100 times that amount to correct if the correct information is only learned from field results during the active construction or realization phase of the project. This should illustrate the extreme importance that development plays in ensuring the quality and profitability of products, services and plant. Development has phases through which it must pass to ensure that the best results are obtained at the end of the day.

The first phase is the basic assessment or study where the concepts and their feasibility can be studied, examined and tested under practical circumstances. Facts and statistics concerning these systems or products should be obtained from functional and operational systems and plants which can be used as benchmarks or references. From this information the whole development process can progress to the conceptual design of a prototype, or a feasibility study of the concept.

Dale and Oakland (1993) state that the quality of design is determined by:

- the degree to which the functional requirements have been expressed in the design;

- the degree to which the specification requirements have been realized;

- the degree to which the design permits rational production and marketing (and for many projects, permits construction or erection);

- the efforts made to attain a reasonable life (or failure rate) with low maintenance costs;

- the speedy feedback of new experience and quality troubles.

Senior management are responsible for ensuring that the customer's needs and the other project objectives are fully integrated into the development and later the design activities. This is necessary in order to ensure that the development and design progressively and continuously meet the customer's and project's quality needs and requirements.

The final phase of development is the feasibility study, using the literature or prototypes, which can supply the best information available. It is also important to note that during the activity many test variations and combinations have to be considered under the worst possible operating conditions in order to determine the most realistic as well as the worst possible scenarios. A pre-feasibility study may be needed to demonstrate that the design and the concepts are feasible. After this study it is usually appropriate to go into the first phase of a full feasibility study.

Here, as far as possible, benchmark units and systems or sub-systems are reviewed and used as inputs for the feasibility study. Out of the feasibility study phase flows an approved, initial design concept.

It is important to note that throughout all these phases, all sessions of brainstorming or discussion of basic concepts, together with all the assumptions, must be clearly documented for ease of review at a later stage.

In order to obtain the assurance that the quality, i.e. the conformance to requirements and deliverables of the facility developed in the feasibility study are met, a review must be made as to whether products or services will satisfy the market requirements. The analysis should highlight possible commercial and engineering risk areas, and give information that will allow further correction so that the risks are as small as possible, thus creating an acceptable product, service and facility for producing them for the market within budget and time constraints.

However, any development or design review becomes very difficult if the basic, underlying information has not been properly documented for ease of traceability and use. It is impossible to develop a facility without learning everything about it first, and without the desired 'top down review' of the design through a development study review and through modifying and minimizing design errors. It is extremely important that, during these activities, these reviews are carefully documented, along with the reasons and the results of any design changes flowing out of these reviews.

The development of a feasibility study for a facility to produce products must include many parameters. These include:

Reliability

This is the probability that a plant or system will perform the required function, under given conditions, for a given period of time. Reliability, therefore, involves six factors:

- The expression and quantification of the probability of failure.

- The definitions and requirements for product performance (these usually improve the deliverables of the product).

- The use of the product or system.

- The time between failures, including the frequency of routine maintenance.

- The environmental situation and conditions in which the system or facility has to serve.

- The ease and simplicity with which a facility and service can be maintained and kept in working order, so that its availability to the user, under a wide variety of separate conditions, will still be ensured. This is also an important factor to consider in the facility development phase.

Maintainability

Development must also take account of maintainability and the economics of maintenance so that ultimate designs, which are maintenance-friendly, can be produced. Systems and materials which do not need high maintenance attention or which are not prone to failure should also be developed and used wherever possible and feasible.

Safety

The system or facility must be intrinsically safe and preferably fail-safe. This includes ergonomics, which can play an extremely important role, as there is a direct correlation between safety, user-friendliness and ergonomics. The system or facility that fatigues the user is generally regarded by users as being inferior because all the quality requirements of that facility have not been met, because quality is still a people's business and is experienced by the users long after the product or facility has been designed and constructed.

Manufacturability/constructability

Development for manufacturability or constructability is extremely important so that reliable, easy-to-manufacture, non-process-sensitive systems and facilities can be developed and designed. The easier it is to manufacture or construct, the less chance there is of manufacturing or construction errors. The quality of the manufactured product will be higher with fewer variations when quality principles are employed. For example, the use of aluminium in designs where it had to be joined by welding was avoided by some designers because of the perceived weldability problems of the metal.

Quality management and control during construction

During the development phase it is also necessary to establish what the required quality management and control levels, standards and procedures will have to be. This is necessary to ensure and demonstrate that a product or service that has been created, can be controlled and managed in terms of conformance to all the prerequisites of the deliverables.

Failure analysis

Ultimately, at the end of the development process, it is necessary to do a failure mode and effect analysis or a fault-tree analysis on the plant or facility that has been developed to ensure that the opportunities for error and variation are reduced to a statistically acceptable minimum for the new facility or product. Dale and Oakland (1994) give further guidance on the performance of fault-tree analysis. This analysis is quite often done by an outside design audit team who are supported by some of the technical personnel that will ultimately run the plant.

Desensitization of critical parameters

It is also important that during the development stage the ultimate product that has been developed is 'desensitized' with regards to critical parameters, because the more critical parameters there are to be controlled in a facility or a service, the more opportunities for failure or breakdown exist.

This discipline leads to the process of design and development for a robust facility or service. Robust here does not necessarily mean large or clumsy, but rather insensitive to or able to tolerate variations and environmental changes or shock, so that the facility is able to carry on functioning satisfactorily, even under short periods of severe operating conditions.

The use of Taguchi methods

No section on quality and development of products and systems would be complete without mentioning the methods developed by Genichi Taguchi, a noted Japanese engineering specialist. He developed advanced quality engineering technologies to reduce failure modes on the one hand, and also to enhance on the other, the effectiveness of development of facilities, products and services and to be able to do this more thoroughly in shorter periods of time.

This section is only intended to make the reader aware of the value and importance of these methods. Should they be required, the reader would be advised to refer to Taguchi's books and publications in order to study them further. Disney and Bendell in *Managing Quality* (Prentice Hall) give further insights into the use of his methods.

Taguchi based his system on three fundamentals:

- The first principle is that of the total loss function. Taguchi takes the modern concept of 'value added for quality' and turns this around and looks at it in terms of the loss imparted to society from the time the product or facility is shipped or supplied, to the time it is ultimately out of use. It quantifies the loss to society as a result of the use of this product or service as a whole. Disney and Bendell also state that the Taguchi methodology may be applied as off-line quality control in the design stage, or less commonly, as on-line quality control during production.

  It is, therefore, aimed at minimizing these losses and ensuring that the utilization of the product or service does not adversely affect society. Clearly, it does not include losses to society during manufacture of the product or service that the facility produces, and requires the collection and analysis of case study data to establish where these losses are and how, through quality management, they can be minimized and eliminated.

  It is important to note that Taguchi characterized the process capability independently from specification limits, and uses specification limits more as tentative cut-off points than actual indications of the process capability. To those well versed in statistics this appears a very obvious conclusion, but to many in industry, even today, specification and tolerance limits are seen as process capability, while, in essence, the two factors are essentially divorced. They are, however, related when producing a product or service.

- The second principle that Taguchi uses in his methods is in the design of products or facilities. This will be detailed in the third section of this chapter. He generally identifies three stages in product facility or service design: the product facility or service design itself; the process realization design whereby the process ensures that the product facility or service can be produced and delivered correctly and reliably every time; and the actual production operation.

It follows from this that the more effectively quality is designed into a product at the stage where changes and corrections are relatively cheap and easy to make, the less critical on-line or production quality control becomes.

Taguchi breaks down the achievement of quality during the 'off-line' stage into system design, parameter design and tolerance design.

Disney and Bendell (1994) also state that 'at the system design stage, parts and materials are selected and possible product parameter levels for product design are determined while decisions are taken on the selection of equipment and possible levels of process factors'.

During the parameter design stage (which is regarded as the critical step) the nominal factor levels selected by system design are tested. The objective of this stage is to determine product parameters and process-operating levels that are least sensitive to changes in environmental levels and other uncontrollable factors. It is during this stage that robustness is designed into the product or service.

The tolerance design stage further reduces the opportunity for variation by understanding and tightening the tolerances on those parameters which during parameter design and testing have shown that they are critical and can have a large impact on, or are sensitive to, variation. In his design of products, Taguchi emphasizes the importance of achieving robustness during design and the prevention of problems by getting products or services that will be able to stand up to adverse operation and environmental conditions. It is also equally important that the cost during production and operation be known and controls be placed on these.

- The third principle in Taguchi's method is reduction in variation. Here emphasis is placed on a continuous quality improvement process in order to reduce variation in key product performance characteristics. Continuous quality improvement is also aimed at reducing costs in a broader, more philosophical approach than only product performance and establishment.

However, the Taguchi methods are not the be-all and end-all of design and they are not the solution to every design and development situation. Disney and Bendell [1994] state that 'the most important skill remains in knowing when to apply Taguchi and when to employ another method'.

Design planning

The design of a system, product, service or facility is too important to be left to the designer alone. It has to be thoroughly thought through and planned by management. This is especially important on projects where there are many interfaces and interrelating activities and systems.

The planning of the design must identify these up front and the design teams should be established in such a manner that a holistic overview can be taken and thereafter the design broken down into logical sub-sets. The responsibilities, design scope and results or deliverables required should be carefully and formally defined and assigned. This forms the basis of the design brief. This must also include design duties and activities to be performed outside the organization or project team on a contract basis.

This activity is extremely important in achieving quality of design, because, in the author's experience, it is at the design interfaces that omissions and problems often occur. The various designers or design teams often do not design the interface aspects properly and assume that the other will attend to the matter, and it consequently falls between the two. The design management team who are responsible for planning the design activity are responsible for ensuring complete coverage of interface aspects.

CASE STUDY

During the design of a refinery in South Africa, the liaison and management of the various design groups were ineffective. A very basic issue such as the obtaining of the actual rainfall figures for the site in question was not thoroughly checked. The rainfall figure for the site was obtained from the nearest weather station which was only 11 km from the site. However, certain geographic changes between the site and the weather station meant that the rainfall at the site was almost double that received by the weather station. This fact was well known to the farmers who farmed around the site. Furthermore the vegetation also indicated a higher rainfall situation.

This fact was not established by the conceptual designers of the plant layout and therefore not passed on to the team designing the earthworks and drainage, nor were the earthworks or civil contractors made aware of the situation. The end result was that massive earthworks were undertaken simultaneously on the whole of the site. The design called for the almost exclusive use of closed underground stormwater drains. The decision was taken to install them after the terracing was complete, but while the soil had not yet been stabilized.

The rains came and consequently almost all the drains installed at that stage were filled with mud and soil and had to be dug out and replaced at great expense. The civil contractors, instead of the design team, made enquiries with the local farmers and when they had established the rainfall pattern, it revealed unusually high figures recorded in the form of heavy downpours, over and above the rainfall originally designed for. This led to a total reappraisal of the layout design and installation plan.

The suggested preferred approach would have been larger drains, possibly with certain key open ditches which could be cleaned of silt. The sequence of installation would have been to work from lowest to highest levels and ensuring a more stable soil situation before continuing to the next terrace. The contractors and their teams executing the design said that had they been aware of this situation, they would have insisted on certain conceptual design changes that would have avoided, or at worst reduced the problem to acceptable levels.

This site ultimately inherited a problematic drainage situation when heavy rains fell. Problems caused by a lack of quality live on long after the completion dates and last payments have been forgotten. This oversight and lack of interface communication by management also caused major schedule and cost overruns.

The design team can therefore not work in isolation from the other disciplines. This is not only with regard to design interfaces, but is also applicable to the people who have to execute the design as well as operate and maintain the facility that is being designed. The design phase should be regarded as a project in its own right, which has an ultimate 'deliverable' which is the completed, fully specified, reviewed and approved design. This design should be able to be communicated effectively to any competent third party, be it for design review or design execution.

The principle of work breakdown structure is also applicable to the planning of a design with specific milestones forming key elements in this approach. It is often necessary to break the various design processes into their separate elements, as each of these can require different combinations of skills to realize.

These two structures can be presented on a bar chart (see Figure 4.1) which lists the various milestones as well as process elements against time. It is important to include the various design review activities in this chart as these are an integral part of the planning of the design. Many organizations take this chart and add to it the procedures and specifications that are applicable to each activity, as well as sign off spaces for successful completion of each, which convert it to a quality plan or route card for each design milestone or process. These route cards can accompany the design documentation through the design process as a 'traveller' or route card. This information illustrates that all the aspects that affect the quality of the design have been addressed, which facilitates the design review and approval at a later stage.

The amount of effort that a thorough design review requires must never be underestimated. The extent of the review is dependent on the product or service application, as well as design complexity and extent of innovation being introduced. The track record of the design or similar designs, together with the degree of standardization, will also play a role in determining the thoroughness of the design review.

The British standard BS 7000 shows the idealized design process as one that has four major activities after the feasibility study, namely conceptual, embodiment, detail and manufacture design stages.

The term 'embodiment design' may be new to some readers, while the other terms are well known. Embodiment design is a structured development of the concept to ensure that no important issues fall through the net. This is very important if a design of acceptable quality is to be realized. This stage helps to eliminate design uncertainty and completes the design lay-out. The initial modelling is usually completed so that full-scale models or modelling can be carried out to establish any areas of uncertainty. A full review at the completion of this stage is usually advised.

Dale and Oakland in *Managing Quality*, 2nd edition (Prentice Hall, 1994) list four major features that play a role in the quality of a design:

FIGURE 4.1 Idealized design process

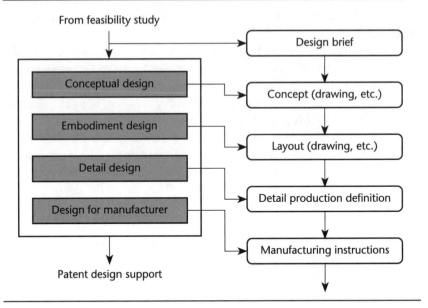

Source: BS 7000 (1989)

- avoid unnecessary complexity;
- avoid unnecessary variety;
- avoid unnecessary costs;
- eliminate features known to cause quality problems.

Quality and the design process

The first steps

The design process is activated when a specific problem has to be solved. The concept of quality relates to how well the problem has been tackled and how holistically effective the solution is. There are certain basic questions that should be asked in order to manage the process successfully so that an optimal design can be achieved.

It is necessary to start the process by accurately identifying and documenting the need that the design has to meet. This will also include accurate problem or opportunity definition. It is advisable, at the end of this activity, to independently review and approve the formulation of the needs, problems and opportunities, because any errors that occur here can be carried through all the activities of the process that follows. This review forms the first quality check in the design process.

The design concept and quality

The next step is to decide whether a new design is necessary, or whether there is an existing proven product or system that can be used or modified (with permission) in order to meet the need.

Oakley in *Design Management* (Blackwell, 1990) states that there should be scope for considerable lateral thinking at this point in the process. Pressures to move quickly at this stage in a project are always very high, and this is the time when a cool head should counter these pressures in order to search out the optimal solution. In many instances elegant solutions to these problems already exist and the ultimate design effort may only be one of identifying the best existing solution and interface modification in order to achieve successful integration into the rest of the system. This activity can save many design hours and is an important link in the chain of events needed to arrive at a 'quality' solution to the problem, i.e. meeting the need of the customer (and stakeholder) in the most mutually beneficial manner.

Influence of design constraints on quality

From the above mentioned it will be seen that the decision to embark on a design process is a major one, and the needs of the design process should be fully understood. It is also necessary to understand what the constraints are that will influence the design. There are both external and internal constraints.

The major external constraints are the needs of the customer and the stakeholders. However, in today's changing world safety, health and the environment, as well as legislation, could also form important external constraints. Oakley (1990) also gives a list of role-players that can have an influence and thus impose external constraints on the design process.

The ability to execute a manufacture or design is an important constraint which could be either internal or external and must always be kept in mind. A design which is difficult, expensive or time consuming to manufacture will inevitably lead to quality problems with the final product or service.

Internal constraints usually lie within the organization performing the design. These can vary from individuals' 'private agendas' wishing to influence the design for their own reasons, to the need to integrate the design into the remainder of the facility. All of these constraints have to be managed carefully so that the human or personal constraints do not negatively affect the design while the more technical and economic restraints are not overlooked, resulting in an inferior design.

The design brief and quality

The importance of design in achieving quality is well-known and ISO 9001 illustrates this very clearly. It is therefore necessary that the design team knows what is expected of them, and that the design task be managed as a project in its own right. The achievement of a good quality of design, i.e. a design that meets the needs of the customer and the stakeholders, is only possible if a thorough design brief has been prepared, independently reviewed and approved. This is the next step in achieving quality through design.

The design brief should be thorough yet concise and should cover two main areas, namely the product or service brief, and the project or resources brief.

The product brief should typically address the following:

- list of customer and stakeholder needs;

- final deliverables required;

- approval and testing requirements;

- special operational, safety, health and environmental requirements and features;

- key milestones in the execution of the design;

- intermediate review requirements;

- areas of design uncertainty;

- logistic and configuration control requirements;

- life expectancy of the item or system;

- list of skills that will be required to realize this brief;

- cost and time constraints;

- statutory requirements;

- aesthetic requirements or constraints;

- ergonomic factors.

A product brief should also identify and classify certain of the key parameters into mandatory, critical, major or minor. This list may vary as the design proceeds and as certain features are included in the design, but it is necessary to establish and convey as much information as is practical to the design team in the product brief.

The aesthetics of a design play an increasingly important role, especially where environmental or ecological issues have also to be taken into account. A design which may be quite acceptable functionally but which may appear offensive to the viewer or may cause an ecological disturbance can often cause problems with the project stakeholders at a future date and reflect badly on the design and the project as a whole. The influence of the quality of the design lives on long after the design process has been completed.

Ergonomics play an important role in the long-term operability and maintainability of the product or service, as well as in the quality of the design. The project brief should list the items, resources and constraints that will influence the execution of the product brief by the design team. This brief will list the needs and milestones that the design project has to meet if it is to be a success.

The project brief will typically address the following.

Resources

- financial constraints and budget;

- time constraints and target dates for specific milestones as well as completion dates;

- design skills required in terms of directly available skills as well as skills that need to be hired in;

- design management skills which will include quality and quantity of people for planning – scheduling, budgeting and cost control, co-ordination, interface management, progress review and, especially important for quality, design review skills;

- environmental and ecological factors;

- the level of conformance to the quality plan;

- the management of the availability and timing of skills and resources.

The design project brief must also include the following:

- configuration requirements and information for document storage and control;

- logistic support such as accommodation, equipment, software and any other special support needed.

Both the product as well as the project brief need to be formally reviewed and approved prior to issue.

Selection of the design brief drafting team

A design brief will only be as good as the team selected to draft it. The person who will manage the design project should lead this team, and typically the team should have the following skills at its disposal.

- project management;

- design skills;

- all the relevant technologies;

- financial support;

- planning;

- quality;

- customers, including operating and maintenance skills;

- stakeholders (major only when practical);

- a representative of the design reviewing team.

Review and approval of the brief

Errors in the design brief will inevitably flow through to the design and ultimately the product, service or facility. The cost of correction of an error in the design brief is very low in comparison to correcting it during design or even after the product or facility has been produced. An independent, objective and critical review and ultimate formal approval of the design brief is essential.

The review team should, as far as possible, be independent and conduct this review formally. The team should consist of representatives from the customer and stakeholder, as well as people with all the technical and managerial skills that the design brief covers, to ensure that the activity is meaningful and adds value to the brief, and at the same time reduces the opportunity for errors to an acceptably low level.

Quality through managing the design process

Quality is influenced by the competence of the design management team

The success of a design project is not only dependent on competent designers, but also on the effectiveness and efficiency of the person or team managing and administering the design project. A good design team will be seriously inhibited from producing a good design if the design project is poorly managed or administered.

Oakley in Chapter 34 of *Design Management* lists the following factors which influence the success of a design project:

- presence or absence of a competent (design) project brief;

- correct prediction of resources (and their deployment) required;

- competent management of project (including ability to work within time, cost and quality restraints);

- quality of working relationships between designers and others both inside and outside the company;

- availability of (sufficient and correct) skills and their effective deployment;

- ability to analyse and respond to changes in specification;

- whether progress reviews are held at appropriate times and correct decisions taken about further work, new directions, or abandonment;

- general quality of project management;

- performance of outside design expertise, if used;

- support interest and influence of top management;

- the correct use of design reviews and audits.

All these elements have an influence on the ultimate quality of the design that is produced, and should be managed correctly if the ultimate design is to be a success and lead to a quality system, product or service.

Managing the design project for quality

The style of management also plays an important role in achieving a successful design that will lead to a quality product or service. The researchers Burns and Stalker (1966) analysed management styles, and even though the work is now dated many of the principles are still valid. They defined two styles, namely a mechanistic style and an organic style.

Mechanistic styles are formal, hierarchical, bureaucratic and inflexible. This style has limited success in design projects, especially where innovative and lateral thinking is required to arrive at good solutions. The organic style usually achieves better results, and is characterized by the following features as discussed by Oakley (1990).

- The common task is the verifying theme and each individual contributes special knowledge and skills.

- Tasks are constantly analysed and redefined as the situation progresses and changes.

- Hierarchy does not predominate: problems are tackled on a team basis.

- Flexibility: jobs are not rigidly or precisely defined. Results or deliverables take precedence.

- Control is through successfully achieving the common goal rather than by institutions, rules and regulations.

- Expertise and knowledge are located throughout the organization, not just at the top.

- Communications consist of information and advice rather than instructions and decisions.

The design management group is usually appointed first, and it is their task to assemble a design team and appoint suitable people. The appointment of such a team will also include design managers and administrators as well as designers, engineers and technicians and an appropriate quality engineer.

The skills required must be established from the design brief and the most suitable, affordable personnel must be found, from inside or outside the organization. A successful track record rather than a 'paper CV' should be sought. Very often it is preferable to form a joint venture between several organizations, each of which is well experienced in a specific skills area or technology. If this option is considered, then a design integrating team or function is also necessary to ensure completeness and continuity, so that a quality design leading to quality products and services can be produced and cross functional issues are taken into account, as indicated by Agnihorthri (1994).

Should it be necessary to use a design consultancy for part or all of the project, then the design management team is cautioned to take special care in the appointment. Previous users of the design consultancy should be consulted to establish the success of the design results. The style of the consultancy, pricing and whether the firm still has the skills (people and systems) that produced the successful results for the previous project must all be taken into account. The financial stability of the consultant is so important that a specific guarantee is often required up front.

There are many other indirect factors that play a role in the success of a design which can affect the quality of the ultimate result. The following is a list of some of the more general factors.

- Accommodation: Is the environment suitable for creative work and will competent designers wish to work there, or will there be a high personnel turnover? The accessibility of other support systems that the design team needs to do a good job cannot be overstressed.

- Configuration control: Does a configuration control system exist so that design records, results and changes can be properly recorded, administered and controlled?

- Customer and design brief information and accessibility: Can the customer or drafter of the design brief be easily contacted for follow-up discussions and review of problematic issues?

- Technical back-up: Are competent technical staff available for advice, and is there access to a suitable library? Is there a suitably equipped drawing office which has modern aids such as computer design facilities, and are suitable test facilities available where prototypes and 'mock-ups' can be tested and proved?

- Links with manufacturing, operations and maintenance: These are important areas of the design. They are often not associated with the final customer and tend to be forgotten. Their input is important if a user-friendly design is to be produced.

Design review and audit – a vital quality tool

In the design quality world one of the most valuable instruments is the independent design review. This may be done in stages throughout a design for a complicated design, or at the end of a more straightforward design. The review can also take the form of a combination of the in-house design and calculation reviews of the designer and his colleagues, together with an external or third party reviewer.

For this reason it is extremely important that the designer clearly documents the design and the associated calculations and design assumptions, etc. in order to leave an information trail for an independent design review. The design reviewer must be able to work through and confirm whether the particular assumptions, input information of the design and a particular design approach are acceptable or not.

Design inputs and outputs must be carefully controlled in this system and design process and output verification are some of the cornerstones for ensuring that the design is acceptable. Design (like development) cannot be made without learning along the road and the need for change and corrections to the design must be catered for. During the project execution certain field errors and failures can be experienced, and the design office must allow for correction of these during this phase.

The control of design changes must take place in a formal, documented and systematic manner. Control of these changes is almost as important as the design itself, because these changes are modifications to the design and they also transmit a lot of information and valuable field experience back into the design process for correction at its core.

It is interesting to note that if the cost ratio of correcting an error at the conceptual and development phase is unity, then at the end of the design phase it could be between five and ten times unity. The ultimate escalation for correction of the error, once the product and service are in use, is often more than a hundred times unity. This shows that the effort expended in design and the control of the quality of the design can give between five to one hundred times the return on effort, in terms of avoiding unnecessary costs and delays later in the project.

It is, therefore, of vital importance that the quality of design is progressively verified. A systematic controlled way of dealing with design inputs, controlling design changes and verifying the design process and output is very important. The control and recording of the lessons learned from the design and changes to the design, are absolutely vital in closing the total quality management loop. Quality that is 'designed in' at this stage, means the avoidance of errors and delay costs later.

It is, therefore, not uncommon for major organizations that do research, development, design and introduction to the market, to spend between 15 and 20 per cent of the budget on these activities. Some even raise it as high as 25 per cent, because this is the phase where the nominally 'cheap effort', in terms of costs and man hours, can have a marked effect later. It is also the front end where well-managed brain power makes the difference between a well-researched, well-understood, developed and designed product, facility or service, and one that has been rushed to a premature completion of all factors which may lead to significant, time consuming and costly corrections later.

The whole design process should be reviewed regularly at suitable milestones so that an independent opinion as to the progressive success can be obtained. Reviews start with the design need and brief and continue through the design inputs and process right up to post-design evaluation and acceptance as well as customer feedback, where necessary.

In some organizations the term 'design review' is used to denote a review of the more technical and operational aspects of the design. This can sometimes take the form of a full technical audit where even the process technology, compatibility and manufacturing facilities are checked, evaluated and comprehensively reviewed.

The term 'design audit' is often used in a broader sense, and will review or analyse the total return (or return potential) that the design and the resources it will employ can realize, i.e. will the design be economically viable. Both of these processes must be carefully and systematically employed to ensure that the requirements of the design brief are met and that quality is designed into the product or service.

An important aspect of the design review is a critical appraisal of the assumption, underlying principles, and input information on which both the design brief and the design are based. Two types of design audit (more holistic) are suggested.

- A pre-project audit to evaluate the estimated resources needed to achieve the design brief results and to make sure that the original estimates are correct, and that the resources can be made available affordably. Any problems in this area usually lead to shortcuts. Experience with shortcuts is that they are always at the expense of quality, either by inadvertent omission or deliberate avoidance.

   This audit should report on the chance of success of the design project as planned so that only viable design projects are considered.

- A full across-the-board audit of all design projects, which reviews the success of the results and the resources employed and needed to complete the design project. These should be conducted every six to twelve months or at the completion of a critical milestone. This will enable the design management to keep the design results, progress and costs on track and within schedule and budget.

The results of a design audit will not only be expressed in terms of non-conformances or 'findings' but also in hard bottom line financial terms. The cost of achieving and executing the design needs to be estimated and equated to the return that the design will give, in order to make sure that it is economically viable. It must be accepted that there will be errors, and acceptable margins of error must also be formulated.

ISO 9001 gives valuable guidelines on design review principles and indicators. In ISO 9001 (the international quality system model), design control is regarded as an extremely important function and a whole section is devoted to it. In this section the planning and development of design are clearly specified and it is advocated that the design activity should be assigned to competent people with a proven track record for that type of design. It must be accepted that not all designers are infinitely qualified or suitable to design all products, facilities and services, and that designers with suitable qualifications and experience should be carefully chosen, so that their skills and experience are suitable for the design task.

A quality design must always be an economically viable design:

- safe to use and maintain;
- economically viable;
- evironmentally and ecologically acceptable;
- user friendly;
- maintenance friendly;
- ergonomically acceptable;
- aesthetically acceptable;
- sociologically acceptable.

Quality in design

The term 'design' is often misconstrued and thought of only in terms of basic drafting and supplying drawings for further conceptual development, fabrication or construction.

Essentially, 'design' means communication, arranging information relating to the design concepts in an orderly way in order to make the information practically applicable and usable, so that a facility, product or service of value can be produced by people, other than the designer, using the information that the designer transmits in the design.

It is evident that the designer needs input from research, development and feasibility studies for a clear understanding of what the end results and requirements of the deliverables should be. Conformance to these requirements will be the confirmation of the success of the design.

The information available to the designer is in many forms and could come in the form of approved manuals, schedules, published data and literature, or validated information from research and development projects or operational benchmark plants. Designers also have an important store of information, in existing data banks, of operating knowledge and equipment. It can be used as design benchmarks which, by virtue of the results of the operational experience, carries validated answers and principles that are credible, and can be used in the design process.

The design is the stage in which concepts, principles and basic information are crystallized into usable facts that any other suitably trained and competent person can take and convert into a product, facility or service.

In the design process, it is important that the opportunities for error be identified, 'designed out' and avoided. The ability of a particular design to be able to handle adverse operating and environmental conditions, without losing its ability to function, is of paramount importance and is broadly referred to as the robustness of the design, which is perceived by the customer as part of the quality of the design.

It is imperative that the design is for the actual use, and not the designers' concept of the intended use. Therefore, it is necessary that designers establish the requirements for the deliverables from the feasibility study and its resultant project scope and design brief very carefully, not in terms of what is easy for them to design or what they think should be designed, but for what is actually required.

Once the deliverables and the requirements and specifications thereof have been established, the conceptual design phase can be commenced and this is where alternative, detailed designs and concepts should be formulated, critically reviewed and evaluated so that the optimum can be selected. After the optimum option has been selected, reviewed and approved, the detail design can commence. It can, however, happen that a concept which has progressed to detail design, shows serious problems and difficulties. The concept may then have to be aborted and the conceptual design phase partially or totally repeated.

Topalian (1994) also indicates that it is important for the quality of design that the designer documents the design clearly. This includes assumptions (what the concepts are); areas of uncertainty (if any); areas of the design which are combinations of other known designs; and areas of the greatest opportunity for weakness or sensitivity to variation (i.e. the least robust aspects of the design), so that any other designer can follow his or her written thoughts through the design, description and documentation phase and understand the concepts, underlying principles and assumptions that the designer has put into the design.

Designers must realize that the design as visualized can only be understood by other people if the design is comprehensively communicated, not only by way of drawings, flow diagrams, etc., but also by way of specifications, and where necessary, procedures and special instructions to ensure that the design intent can be clearly read and understood by a competent third party. Communication of information by a designer should also include manuals for operation, maintenance and, where applicable, even for erection, assembly and testing.

CHAPTER FIVE

Human factors affecting quality in projects

The quality 'mind-set' in projects

Projects are usually time and money driven, and very often these driving factors overrule the objective of completing a functional facility that will satisfy the owner and operator for the full life of the plant. Consequently, the concept of life-cycle quality is often not built in from the very beginning.

Many of the people working on a project are of necessity contract workers, by the very nature of the limited life-span of the project. These people's motivation is essentially mercenary in nature and they are there to get the job done as quickly as possible in order to receive their money and move on to the next job. This approach usually means that any task requiring extra effort or time is either avoided or watered down to a no-nuisance level, and this can have an adverse effect on the systematic, planned, trained, organized and controlled way of working that any 'right first time' quality job would require.

In cases where reputable contracting or contract management organizations are employed, this problem is reduced. If a project sullies their reputation it adversely affects their ability to successfully tender on other contracts.

Often the need for quality is not understood by smaller sub-contractors who survive by their wits, and generally operate in a more informal manner and business environment. The mind-set of many of these operators is 'this is how we always do things' and the customers (the next stage in the project) have to be satisfied with what they get.

The mind-set is often one of 'let's get the plant finished in time and any latent defects will be somebody else's problems at a later stage', that is, after the contractors have left the site and moved on to another job.

Negotiate and agree on quality from the very start

Effective quality is negotiated into the contract and under the best circumstances a contractor will give the quality that the contract stipulates. If quality has not been carefully and comprehensively 'contracted into' the project during the contract negotiation stage, then it is almost impossible to instill it after the contract has been signed.

One of the best ways of dealing with the syndrome that 'quality problems are somebody else's problems, tomorrow', is to establish a pro-quality approach and culture (work ethic) right from the contract negotiation stage. The principle of only paying for completed work that conforms to the contractual quality requirements must also be entrenched. Such establishment and entrenchment of a pro-quality culture can be brought about by quality orientation and training sessions which stress the importance of the particular quality levels and systems on the project. This must be carried out up front, before people are allowed on site or allowed to commence work on components or systems at the sub-contractor's premises.

This 'cultural mind-set' has to be supported by a disciplined and orderly approach to ensuring and assessing compliance with the standards of the work performed for each of the milestones on the project. Typically, this can be done by insisting that contractors and sub-contractors draw up and have quality system plans approved for all important contracts or tasks prior to commencement of the work. This must be followed by progress and final assessment of the work done by both the senior contracting staff or suppliers, as well as the project management personnel, before payment can be made.

The approach is that quality, like justice, must not only be done, but must be seen to be done and must enjoy having a high priority on the project. This may well cost approximately ± 5 per cent more in up-front preparation, but it has been demonstrated to save between 10 and 15 per cent downstream in the elimination of work that has to be repeated, or lost time (let alone lost credibility and prestige).

It is also important that project management does not (or is not perceived to) place quality on the back burner by quality-negating decisions, actions or remarks. Every decision in which the time schedule or cost compromises quality, that is, every decision made in favour of schedule or cost at the obvious expense of quality, sends a strong indirect message rippling through the project to the effect that quality is not an important issue, and that shoddy work or partial completion of milestones is acceptable.

Projects offer limited opportunities for gradual improvement

The uniqueness of every project makes it difficult to employ the techniques of limited, gradual improvement at grass-roots level (Kaizen) that more stabilized manufacturing and service situations can use successfully. Contracting organizations can apply this technique internally to a limited degree, but the task-force approach that is often needed can only allow for this to some extent during the planning stage of the project.

The opportunities that the individual has, at the construction site or in the field, to relay important information that will make improvement possible, are limited. Organizations should create a forum and system for 'listening downwards' which will allow and encourage information and suggestions to flow upwards so that 'hassles' and shortcomings can be discussed and brought out into the open, without the workforce feeling threatened. This is the beginning of worker empowerment, which is a very powerful motivational tool, even in contracting situations.

Many small problems and hassles often demotivate a workforce at the expense of quality which embraces both effectiveness and efficiency: 'do the right things correctly'. The institution of feedback or 'de-briefing sessions' after the completion of a task or upon completion of an activity controlled by a quality plan, can help to air problems, or to highlight instances where things went well. This form of feedback also affords credibility to the importance of the knowledge and skills of the workers, and allows the information that is made available at these sessions to be used for improvement, which is the second important step in the workforce empowerment programme.

A well-run and 'publicly positively responded to' suggestion system can also be very useful. Once again, it must be seen to operate, be impartial, and distribute any rewards, credit or praise openly and fairly.

Training on projects

People who start working on a project, no matter how senior or skilled in their field, will need some form of training or orientation to bring them up to speed on the project quickly and effectively. This principle is also true for training and orientation toward quality and its function and priority on the project.

Training can vary from broad awareness, which everybody must have, to very specific quality training per discipline, trade and operation. This is necessary in order to ensure that everybody on the contract fully comprehends their specific applicable role in doing his/her job properly. Everyone must realize that achieving a totally successful project (of which quality is one of the major items) depends on the part played by every individual.

Tasks can only be performed successfully by people possessing the correct skills. This refers to the knowledge that has been learned and practised until the task can be performed without error. The amateur practises until he/she gets 'it' right, the professional practises until he/she cannot get it wrong.

In the world of projects, as in most other areas of endeavour, it is impossible always to recruit staff that are fully skilled for the range of tasks and variations on tasks that the different projects will require. Training in some or other form will always be required if staff are to be given the skills to perform effectively (quality) and efficiently (productivity). In instances where skilled staff are available, orientation in respect of the specific requirements and peculiarities of the project will invariably be necessary. Very often the orientation process will highlight further training needs.

Lammermeyr (1990) states that 'if we dare to look at the most successful companies in the West today, then we will discover that they, without exception, maintain training departments or centers that are staffed by highly trained individuals who were carefully selected for these important tasks within their own companies'.

The availability and effective utilization of suitably trained and skilled staff is vital to the achievement of quality, schedule and profitability in any organization or project. Lammermeyr also gives the broad requirements for trainers. He illustrates that the quality of training and orientation received can only be as good as the trainer selected, and as the training aids and facilities at his or her disposal.

Training is also an important form of management communication. It is usually applied where the details of management's 'what' and 'how to' in the case of routine operations, have to be communicated, learned and practised.

Section 4 of ISO 9001 (1994) *Quality Systems* highlights the importance of training but gives no indication of how the training needs that are to be met are to be determined. Training needs flow from the need to complement already existing skills in order to be able to perform a task effectively.

The total skills needed to perform a job are usually given in the job description. A job is usually a composite of many individual tasks which are (depending upon their complexity) described in a procedural document or work instruction. The author strongly recommends that a procedural document or work instruction includes not only the activities and equipment/facilities needed, but also describes the skills needed in order to carry out the procedure or work instruction correctly. The totality of skills needed to perform the entire job is therefore the sum of the skills that are specified in all the procedures or work instructions covering a particular job.

It is also necessary to orientate all workers when they join a project team. The peculiarities of the project as well as all other key aspects of their task, together with all management and operational policies and objectives must be made clear to them. Orientation will also be called for with regard to safety, health, hygiene, quality, environmental and other day-to-day matters. All of these are vital for the establishment and maintenance of a focused, motivated and happy workforce. Such a workforce is essential if the dynamic and rapidly-changing situations that typify projects are to be handled successfully.

Projects of a longer duration may often require re-orientation, especially after the attainment of major milestones, at which point the disciplines, direction, technology or pace of the project may have to be changed in order to reach the next set of objectives.

These principles hold true for both contractors and sub-contractors. Often sub-contractors need more orientation and training than the staff of major contractors, because the latter have usually been trained in and/ or exposed to formal quality systems and management styles on projects and have embraced them as part of the organization's culture.

Many organizations see training as a major stumbling block because of added expense incurred and the time it consumes. However, training can vary in duration from a few hours to a few days, depending upon the complexity of the project or system. Experience has shown that if the training that is given avoids even one 're-work' or repair situation on a task or contract, the cost of such training will already have been recovered.

If management feels that training is expensive, consider the cost of ignorance or a lack of skills.

Maintaining quality during the last phases of a project

Is it possible to maintain quality standards during the last phase of a project, when the complement of people working on the project has to be decreased? The answer is 'yes', but this requires very careful management. Rubach (1995) points out that the treatment of staff at this stage of the project is critical. The way in which staff members are treated plays a major role in maintaining the quality standards that are required of a particular project or task.

In the author's personal experience, morale, trust, quality and productivity suffer badly during this phase of any project, as in the case of any company that is downsizing. Very often, the finalization of a project seems to take far longer than was originally planned. The factors mentioned above contribute largely to this problem. Many of the contract workers who do not have other contracts to move on to, drag the project out in order to sustain their income while looking for alternative employment.

There are several ways in which this problem can be dealt with or minimized, namely:

Early release of main contractor

Release the main contractor when about 95 per cent of the project has been completed, and use the client's operation and maintenance staff and a so-called 'mop-up contractor' to finish the final tasks as well as the last phases of commissioning. This solution is not always possible, especially in cases where special technology is involved, and commissioning as well as operational technology transfer training have to be carried out by the main contractor. 'Turnkey projects' can usually not be finished off in this manner, and they are often best addressed by continuing maintenance and service agreements.

Completion bonus

Pay a completion bonus which is the equivalent of three months' project wages in order to make completion by the key contract workers worthwhile. This will give the contract worker the time, after being paid off, to look for other contracts. It is important to link the completion bonus not only to the scope of work, but also to quality and project schedule. This approach will help to reduce the possibility of cost as a result of re-work, coupled with schedule over-runs. It is important that such a bonus be negotiated at the very start of a contract worker's employment discussions, rather than trying to offer it in the dying moments of the project.

Experience has shown that many contract workers start looking for other employment six months before the termination of their contract, which leads to untimely resignations. Keep the permanent as well as the contract staff and workers informed of project progress, and of their probable completion dates. This respects the individual's right to know, because he/she is a stakeholder in the project, and it helps everyone to plan their employment and their lives accordingly.

Transfer of technology

The transfer of technology from the project personnel to the operating and maintenance personnel is vital if all the final 'close out' aspects affecting quality are to be successfully completed. This can be achieved by appointing the respective senior operating and maintenance personnel of the client and/or facility operator at the 60 per cent or 70 per cent completion stage of the project, and making them part of the project team. They will have to 'live with the errors of the contractor'.

There are many instances where it is advantageous to include the senior operation and maintenance staff in the project from the very start.

Cross-level effects

It is important to pay attention to the cross-level effects discussed by Rubach (1995). The correct balance of skills for this phase of the contract must be maintained in order to ensure continuity of capabilities, support systems and services even during the downsizing of the establishment phase. It is vital not to lose key people during this phase, and this is the area in which the completion bonus can play a valuable role.

Contract workers accept that as a specific phase or section of the contract is completed, their contract has run its course and will be terminated. However, if the process of reducing the complement of contract workers is perceived as being unco-ordinated, or if favouritism is suspected, then resistance to this process will occur. Consequently, worker morale, trust and motivation will suffer.

It is also necessary, from time to time, to reduce staff who were perceived to be permanent employees of the main contractor, and the above-mentioned comments also apply in such cases.

The reduction of more permanent project staff has to be carried out with greater care. From the point of view of quality and productivity, the balance of necessary intuitive skills must be maintained after the downsizing operation. Intuitive skills play a very important role in getting any job done optimally. There is no computer program that can replace the intuitive skills of a human being who performs his or her work in an unconsciously competent manner. Individuals who are able to work in this way form one of the cornerstones of a pro-quality culture.

The process of downsizing a project team, especially when personnel are laid off and not merely transferred to another task, is an emotionally stressful time. Rubach (1995) states: 'Next to the death of a relative or a friend there is nothing more traumatic than losing a job.' Under these circumstances, the emotional needs of the remaining staff can be greater than their cognitive needs and they will need special management support and empathy during these times.

Open and honest communication is vital, and if other projects are being negotiated, the dissemination of information concerning these and any opportunities is necessary, wherever possible, in order to create a new vision for the personnel affected. The maintaining of a new vision is very important in order to retain their loyalty and commitment to the organization. Failure to take cognizance of these factors and to address them properly will leave the organization with an angry, depressed and anxious workforce that is unable to perform. The best procedures and training will not correct this problem, because it has its roots in the very issue of downsizing and in how sensitively, sensibly and credibly it was performed. The quality of products or services invariably suffers under these circumstances, or is even non-existent.

As the project progresses, the uncertainty factor regarding where the next job is coming from begins to concern the workforce, especially if other projects are not in the pipeline. Uncertainty is extremely demotivating and leads to a non-focused workforce that is preoccupied with 'finding another job after this one'. In instances where contract personnel are successful in finding alternative contracts, people often leave the project prior to completion at a stage when it is almost impossible to replace them and bring the new incumbent 'up to speed' in time. This untimely loss of skill always affects quality negatively. Many of the people working their notice month become slack and do not give their best. This results in poor quality work, much of which will be difficult to detect by means of normal inspection and test frequencies and procedures.

Summary of methods

The following is a list of some of the techniques that can be used to minimize the problems that can have a negative impact on quality:

- Wherever possible, line up alternative projects or contracts to which staff can proceed after successful completion of the project in hand.

- Pay a bonus to staff who remain until completion of the project.

- Arrange for operations, maintenance and inspection staff of the ultimate owner or operator to start working side-by-side with the contract personnel from the 60 or 70 per cent completion stage.

- Have a small pool of staff who are contracted to stay on for three months after completion of the operation to ensure that all the commissioning and start-up problems are ironed out, and that documentation is completed.

- Have a small team of head-office staff on all key aspects of the project so that there are some staff to whom the pressures of looking for another job do not apply.

The influence of performance bonuses on quality

Introduction comment

The debate regarding the advantages and disadvantages of performance bonuses is by no means settled, and there is merit in both sides of the argument. The author would, however, like to share some of his experiences as these could provide guidance to managers while they try to come to a decision as to whether and what type of bonus is appropriate.

Because of the time constraints that are usually applicable, projects are more demanding of the workforce than are routine tasks. People who are involved in project work usually expect to receive a salary or wage that falls in the upper levels of wages or salaries applicable for their skills or profession. Contract workers often see themselves as 'job mercenaries' and expect to be paid considerably more (up to 30 per cent) than those in permanent employment, in order to compensate them for the times when they are unemployed.

There are occasions when, in spite of these higher wages, it is necessary to offer some form of performance bonus as an added incentive to staff, in order to achieve an objective within a very limited period or under very difficult working conditions. This discussion is not intended to address issues such as 'danger pay', or very high wages paid to special categories of workers (because of market shortages or very special combinations of skills and/or physical abilities required by the task).

A performance bonus must link quantity to quality of output, and failure to meet both sets of criteria must also mean a total forfeiture of the bonus. If the decision to pay bonuses has been taken, then it is advisable to give bonuses to all the members of the team, not construction workers only. The bonus must be structured in such a manner that the peer pressure placed on quality control and assurance staff to accept non-conforming work, material or systems does not become unacceptably high. This problem can be illustrated by the following case study, in which the author was directly involved.

CASE STUDY

A large petrochemical plant was well behind schedule, and the labour productivity had become unacceptably low. The worst hit area was that of site-assembled and finally welded pipe spools. The decision was taken to pay a very substantial bonus to the assembly and welding teams if a certain section of the plant that was on the critical path was completed on a certain date. The achievement of quality was not clearly linked to the result. Longer hours were worked and both progress and output improved. However, within a week the inspection staff reported that short cuts were being taken and that the quality of the completed plant was not in accordance with the design criteria.

The first action was to place pressure on the contractor's inspectorate to be a 'little lenient' in the light of the urgent need for completion. It soon became evident that a 'little leniency' would not do the trick, and a flood of concession requests poured into the project management offices. The number of concession requests was so high that the resolution of the concessions would take too long, and ultimately the inspectors were threatened with violence by their workmates and a non-payment of their bonus by supervisory management. Several of the men succumbed to the pressure and the plant was finished on time, 'warts and all'.

The question arises whether the inspection standards were not too high originally, and in some instances they were actually lowered. However, when that section of the plant had to be commissioned, the commissioning took more than two and a half times as long as planned, because many repairs to correct defective workmanship had to be undertaken before commissioning could finally be achieved. The cost of the correction of 'non-quality' in this case exceeded the money saved on wages and penalty clauses by 250 per cent. These results speak for themselves, and confirm that the correct balance between schedule, cost and quality is a very important one.

CASE STUDY

A pipe spool fabrication facility had chosen a fast but unreliable welding technique in order to achieve a very difficult schedule target. The standard approaches to welding procedure and welder competence establishment, approval and coding were rushed through and approval to proceed with production was given 'under concession'.

The welding reject rate after non-destructive examination started at 60 per cent of welds performed and was gradually forced down to 40 per cent, but could not be lowered further. Production was stopped after six weeks and specialists were brought in in order to qualify the process properly, as well as to re-train the welders in the new procedures. An eight-week delay resulted, but once production was resumed, the reject rate ran at 5 per cent.

It was decided to pay the welders a cash production bonus which was linked to the quality of the output. Within two weeks, the gains in productivity at the acceptable quality level disappeared. An examination of the situation indicated that more than 70 per cent of the welders that received the bonus on Friday were either not at work on the following Monday or were so hung over from a weekend's drinking that they could not work effectively. The bonus was modified to a hamper of almost 75 per cent of the original value and the remainder in cash.

The hamper was filled in such a way that the welder received something for his wife or girlfriend such as perfume, talcum powder or bath salts, something for his children, usually in the form of popular sweets and toys. The area where the plant was situated was a wine-drinking region and a single bottle of good wine was added to the hamper. The gains were re-established within three weeks of instituting this type of bonus. There was also an added advantage that only became evident after several months, namely that the second form of bonus gained the receiver recognition for his achievement in the eyes of his family. This ultimately resulted in family pressure for him to perform well, as they were benefiting directly from the bonus.

Putting together the correct contents of the hampers required more up-front effort by the personnel and pay offices in order to determine the size and composition of the individual's family, and to fill the hamper with appropriate items. This approach gave recognition to the worker and assured him that he was not just a number on a payroll but a real, unique person with specific needs. It also improved relationships between the contract management and workers.

Summary of some of the approaches

Summary of some of the successful approaches to the paying of bonuses on projects:

- pay a bonus for successful, acceptable completion of milestones;

- do not include quality assurance and quality control staff in the production bonus scheme;

- include the necessary documentation as an integral part of every milestone;

- if bonuses have to be paid to Quality Assurance (QA) and Quality Control (QC) staff, link these to successful commissioning of the facility;

- tailor the bonus for the work situation, as a money-only type of bonus can lead to the type of problems described in the Case Study above.

CHAPTER SIX

The application of quality management principles to cost engineering

Introduction

Quality as defined in this book can also be applied to cost engineering with an important clarification, namely that the cost engineer serves 'internal customers' more often than external customers. It is also important to realize that satisfying an internal customer or the next department that must use the outputs of the cost engineer, is just as important as satisfying an external customer. The universal principles of management that result in good quality can also be applied to the principles of cost engineering in order to build quality into this important service.

'Cost engineering' can be defined as the application of scientific principles and techniques to problems of expenditure, estimation, cost control and profitability (courtesy of the American Association of Cost Engineers). There are strong parallels between cost and quality engineering and these can be used to advantage in order to improve an already valuable management tool.

The generic application of quality management to cost engineering

If quality management principles are to be applied to cost engineering, then it is important to identify the need that gave rise to the necessity for a cost engineer and the cost engineering discipline or service. Project management needs timely warning and proper advice based on scientific and technical insights into project costs, which will enable them to take appropriate corrective action where necessary.

In this approach cost engineering can be compared to an overall engineering audit of the project, but with a future perspective.

All work is a process which must occur in a planned and organized manner in order to give an end result or deliverable that will satisfy the need that initiated the work in the first place. Cost engineering is also a process that must occur in an orderly manner in order to satisfy the same need. The customer who has this 'need' is project management, and the deliverable that will fully satisfy the need is timely warning and proper advice giving insight into technical problems (or information) relating to project costs, bringing about appropriate corrective action, or even providing information that project costs are under control and within budget.

A deliverable or service of this nature is very comprehensive and needs to be broken down into more specific project-related deliverables. These need to be measured and controlled in order to satisfy both the project engineer (the first customer) and project management (the second customer) that the specific deliverables (usually information and recommendations) are of acceptable quality, i.e. will fully satisfy the need timeously and affordably.

The requirements and specifications against which the deliverables are to be measured and controlled must also be established and mutually agreed between the supplier (the cost engineer) and the customer (project management).

From this approach it will be seen that the supplier (the cost engineer) must work backwards through the whole 'process model', i.e. from customer need, to deliverable, to requirements and specifications, to the process or activities that can establish or create the deliverables, right back to all the inputs that need to be processed or that are used by the process and therefore need to be controlled, thereby ensuring credibility and applicability.

From the definition of quality, it will be seen that quality by implication means getting it right every time. This requires competent people using a system, methods, controls and assessment that will ensure that work is done correctly every time, not by reactive correction, but by pro-active prevention of errors through planning the use of a suitable system and method, measurement of results, correction of errors and ultimately continuous (gradual) improvement.

The fundamental principle of quality means that every input must be correct and credible and every work stage, activity or operation in the process must occur correctly. The work process or activity must be monitored or measured to enable continuous control and/or timeous appropriate correction in order to make sure that all the activities occur correctly, traceably and credibly every time. Every output must also be measured or assessed for full compliance with all the requirements and specifications to ensure prevention and where necessary, timeous detection and correction of errors, so that they cannot be passed down the line, or continuously repeated inadvertently.

Quantification of the use of the quality management principles in cost engineering

If this philosophy is embraced and applied to cost engineering, it can be illustrated by means of the process model (see Figure 2.1 and Table 6.1).

The cost engineering detail of the columns in Figure 2.1 are customized and given in Tables 6.2 to 6.4, but working in reverse from the deliverables to the inputs. Table 6.2 is a list of typical cost engineering deliverables and the type of controls needed to establish whether they are acceptable to both the cost engineer and the various customers. Table 6.3 lists some of the typical cost engineering processes and their controls that need to be employed in order to convert acceptable inputs into acceptable outputs and/or deliverables.

Table 6.4 lists some of the inputs that a cost engineer needs in order to be able to perform his/her work successfully. This also includes the measurement or checks and controls needed to confirm that the inputs are acceptable. This does not take the responsibility away from the supplier of the input to supply an acceptable item that conforms to the cost engineer's requirements.

The cost engineer is the customer of the supplier of the input information or statistic (be they internal or external) and the customer must specify what his/her deliverables, requirements, specifications, controls and measurement methods are, in order to receive, monitor and control inputs every time, otherwise 'garbage in will be garbage out'. It is important to note that in Table 6.4 these are expressed generically and will need to be made project and deliverable specific.

If these tables are studied, it can be concluded that this is no more than a holistic view of managing the cost engineering process carefully, as it is intended to be.

It is the firm belief of the author that if one looks after good management, quality will look after itself. This is a deliberate attempt at avoiding a 'hard quality sell' and to illustrate that all the quality or 'performing the job well' aspects of cost engineering can generally be formulated in known cost engineering terms and language. The holistic systematic, planned and disciplined approach to doing the job properly on time for the customers (be they internal or external), is what quality is all about.

The cost engineer must establish for him/herself that the inputs are known, agreed and credible. It is also important to pro-actively decide upon the best cost engineering processes and procedures for the circumstances, and that these always occur in a controlled and measurable manner (even if the measures are approved documents or a traceability trail, etc.). The outputs of the cost engineering process are the credible (as measured and demonstrated) deliverables, that the customer wants in order to satisfy a specific need timeously and affordably. These needs are usually information on which management can make decisions regarding the use of financial resources on the project.

An important control and communication method for these systems is the use of approved procedures which communicate the desired way in which the system and its sub-activities are to be managed and operated.

Finally, and probably the most important aspect, is that the cost engineer must make proposals or suggestions to management to solve cost related problems which have arisen or could arise during the execution of the project. The onus rests on the project management to accept these proposals and act upon them or not.

Table 6.5 gives a list of the typical minimum 'identification information' that should be included on appropriate documentation to ensure traceability or an audit trail for maintenance and control of the identification and credibility of information from a cost engineering point of view.

If the project is large enough it can establish its own stationery on which the routine information can be permanently printed. The other information will have to be stored, in a specific area or space provided. The advantage of a pre-printed form is that it also serves as a memory jogger for the information required.

Many projects program this information as part of the standard document format into the computers used on the project and provision is made automatically.

TABLE 6.1 The cost engineering 'quality process model'

Inputs	→ Control of Inputs	→ Process & Process Control	→ Control of Outputs	→ Outputs to Customers
Cost engineering (CE) skills	Establish credibility of all these before they can be used for the process.	Use inputs to supply data and information for the CE process to obtain the desirable outputs and deliverables. Some typical process actions are:	Keep processes under control for credible outputs.	Cost estimate of pre-feasibility study.
CE procedures			Assess credibility of outputs before forwarding to customer.	Project budget.
CE case studies and bench mark examples	Check credibility or origin of information		Statistically check outputs by alternative methods to ensure continued credibility	Work breakdown structure costs.

TABLE 6.1.2

Inputs	Control of Inputs	Process & Process Control	Control of Outputs	Outputs to Customers
Project scope	Check applicability of tenders to quote. Compare tender evaluation report with invitation to tender lists.	Review project scope. Review and bring work breakdown packages into the system.	Compare costs with similar benchmark projects, parts of projects and/or published figures to obtain relative project situations.	Work packages.
Engineering data sheets				Change order register.
Project estimate		Obtain change order data and process further.		Purchase order evaluation.
Work breakdown structure (WBS)	Have estimates independently reviewed for correctness and credibility.	Obtain cash and cash flow commitments.		

TABLE 6.1 Continued

Inputs	→ Control of Inputs	→ Process & Process Control	→ Control of Outputs	→ Outputs to Customers
TABLE 6.1.3				
Engineering and construction information	Use only the final approved LUBS and WP.	Gather and process project cost data for the cost report.		Cost reports (monthly)
Work packages (WP)	Review abbreviation report for correctness.	Study trends and apply these into the forecast.		Variance reports (monthly)
Deviation from WBS	Review invitation to tender department for completeness.	Analyse cost and supply, etc.		Forecast final cost (monthly)
Deviation from WP		Check and ensure that process procedures are correct, up to date and approved for the project in question.		Proposal on how to get back to budget.
Invitation to tender/quote	Independent review of tender evaluation report for completeness and acceptability by procurement committee which has a QA member.	Ensure that computer programs are applicable, user friendly and free of any form of virus.		
Tenders and quotes		Check that the assumption and models upon which the computer programs were based are applicable or sufficiently applicable to the project in question.		
Tender evaluation report				
TABLE 6.1.4				
Expenditure per cost centre	Expenditure reports to be audited regularly.			
Variation orders	Variation in change order to be reviewed and formally approved.			
Change orders, etc	Payments to be made against authorized signatures/ approval procedures.			
Authorization of final payments				

TABLE 6.2 Deliverables of the cost engineering process

Deliverables	Requirements	Control Measures
TABLE 6.2.1		
Cost estimate of pre-feasibility study	Pre-feasibility report, supporting information and assumptions	Review sources of information against benchmarks and case studies
TABLE 6.2.2		
Project budget	Estimate cost of project activities and materials	Compare with equivalent project benchmarks of broken down activities
TABLE 6.2.3		
Work breakdown structure, costs, work packages	Activities broken down into sufficient detail for all the work elements to follow	Separate review by engineering, design and construction to confirm corrections and completeness of contents
TABLE 6.2.4		
Change order register and system	Details of all change orders	Cross reference with project details for completeness
TABLE 6.2.5		
Purchase order evaluation	Full evaluation forms and information	Compare with invitations to tender and specifications Compare prices of supplied items between quality approved suppliers and others (if applicable) and include in the cost of quality figures
TABLE 6.2.5		
Cost reports (monthly)	Details of costs and claims as they arise (progressively)	Compare costs with contracts and only approve acceptable ones
Variance report (monthly)	Details of variances from standards and schedule	Measure against requirements and schedule
TABLE 6.2.6		
Forecast final cost (monthly)	Information for computer simulation	Review and approval of computer model and program
Proposal on how to get back to budget	Proposal to be feasible and within means of project team	Proposals preferably not to cause slippage of final cost or schedule
TABLE 6.2.7		
Project history records	To be concise, logical and user-friendly	Report to be proofread by a competent third party
Closeout report		
Proposals for final settlement of contracts, etc.	Use original contracts and minutes of negotiation meetings as a basis	No unilateral deviations from original agreements

TABLE 6.3 Typical cost engineering process and methods employed

Process	Requirements	Control Measures
TABLE 6.3.1		
Review project scope Review work breakdown packages	Sufficient detail and input from engineering to review meaningfully	Compare with engineering input and QA approval
TABLE 6.3.2		
Estimate cost of equipment plant Estimate cost of construction Estimate cost of labour Estimate cost of administration Estimate cost of management	Use normal estimation procedures for these parameters	Compare with equivalent published data for similar activities
TABLE 6.3.3		
Obtain and review invitation to tender Review tenders Evaluate case studies and experience in order to formulate action to correct cost overruns Draft project history reports	Standard tender procedures Use computer models and programs for data processing and forecast	Independent review of variance report and final cost forecasts for credibility
TABLE 6.3.4		
Obtain change order data	Customized change order system and procedures	Compare system design with equivalent systems Plot the number of claims being made that are not covered by change orders
Review change order data	System whereby cost detail automatically goes to cost engineer	Check various approvals and compare with contract/order
TABLE 6.3.5		
Obtain costs and commitments Obtain reports on cost of quality		
Draft cost report	Cost report that embraces all the factors needed by project manual	Does this report provide user friendly and credible management information on which decisions can be made?
TABLE 6.3.6		
Draft variance report Forecast final costs	Information for computer simulation and programs	QA on program and computer model, etc.

TABLE 6.4 Inputs for the cost engineering process

	Input	Requirements	Control Measure
6.4.1	Project scope	Project scope detail from engineering and design	Independent review and verification of acceptability
6.4.2	Engineering data sheets	Data sheets giving enough detail for costing purposes	Approved engineering data sheets
6.4.3	Project estimate	Document from feasibility study giving detail estimate, etc.	Review against benchmark or case study equivalents, etc.
6.4.4	Work breakdown structure (approved)	Work broken down into information with sufficient detail to allow a full impression of relevant data and costs	Review against typical published acceptable norms and account credibly for variations
	Project engineering and construction information	Work packages grouped by discipline or 'turn-key' type of job making the work more manageable	Review against typical published acceptable norms and account for variations
6.4.5	Work packages		
	Project engineering and construction information		
6.4.6	Deviations from WBSs		
6.4.7	Deviations from WPs	Deviation reports giving details of deviation and implications	QA review and recommendation of the deviation report, etc.
		Review tenders and change order requests for possible deviations	Log deviations or requests and compare statistics with project norm costs and quality/value of outputs with benchmark projects
6.4.8	Invitation to tender (quote)	Tender invitation documents and specifications	Control that all requirements and specifications are in the tender documents and that tenders for important equipment are only invited from QA approved suppliers
		Reports on acceptability status of firms approved to tender (re capacity, financial stability and quality)	

TABLE 6.4 *Continued*

	Input	Requirements	Control Measure
6.4.9	Tenders or quotations	Tenders or quotations to be sufficiently detailed to enable CE to establish conformance or not	Comments by QA group on acceptability of past performance and quality of system
6.4.10	Tender evaluation report	Full tender evaluation report including vendor acceptability	Evaluate against the approved invitation to tender
6.4.11	Expenditure per contract/order	All expenditure approved to be in sufficient detail for identification and to be routed through CE prior to payment of expenditure for recommendation, etc.	Compare progress payments with agreed contractual milestones and establish whether they are in accordance with the contract. Have all expenditures been supported by supporting documents and signatures confirming achievement of milestones and quality?
6.4.12	Expenditure (project internal)	All expenditure approved to be in sufficient detail for identification and to be routed through CE prior to payment of expenditure for recommendation, etc.	Compare progress payments with agreed contractual 'milestones' and establish whether they are in accordance with the contract. Have all expenditures been supported by supporting documents and signatures confirming achievement of milestones and quality?
6.4.13	Variation orders	Order in sufficient detail to fully review variation for all milestones' costs and quality aspects. Order to be formal and approved	Variation orders to be controlled in the same manner as original order i.e. steps 6.8–6.11
6.4.14	Change orders	To be treated as a separate small contract	To be controlled in the same manner as steps 6.8–6.11
6.4.15	Project history facts	Align facts to project milestones and WBS where necessary	Facts to be able to be substantiated by project records
6.4.16	Final delivery note or invoice, etc.	To be accurate in terms of all detail called up on the original order	Compare delivery note details with original order requirements

TABLE 6.5 Typical minimum identification needed for documents to ensure traceability for an 'audit trail'

The following information as a minimum is usually needed on the cover sheet only:

NAME OF ORGANIZATION:

PROJECT NAME AND NUMBER OR ORDER NUMBER:

DOCUMENT NAME:

DATE OF ISSUE:

REFERENCE NUMBER: (Where it can be found in the files physical and/or electronic)

ISSUE OR REVISION NUMBER:

PAGE NUMBER:

NUMBER OF PAGES: (i.e. Page 7 of 18)

AUTHOR:

SIGNATURE OF AUTHOR:
              APPROVER:

WHERE APPLICABLE, LIST OF PEOPLE TO WHOM THE DOCUMENT WAS CIRCULATED FOR INFORMATION OR COMMENT:

Each subsequent sheet should as a minimum typically contain the following:
PROJECT NAME AND NUMBER
REFERENCE NUMBER
REVISION NUMBER
PAGE NUMBER AND NUMBER OF PAGES

The ability to positively influence the course of costs on a project

The main output of a cost engineer is timeous and usable management information, which will give management insight as to how money and its related resources have been, are and will need to be utilized on the project in order to complete the project within budget, quality and time. This information positively helps project management to influence the course and cost of the project, which has a direct bearing on its success.

The greater the amount of preparation that is put into the contract in the pre-project phase, the greater will be the ability of the contractor and customer to understand the task ahead in a 'holistic manner' and negotiate a meaningful contract which will facilitate control and the positive benefits flowing from it. The inverse of this statement is usually also applicable, with varying degrees of compromise.

OPTION 1: Customer and contractor prepare thoroughly for contract

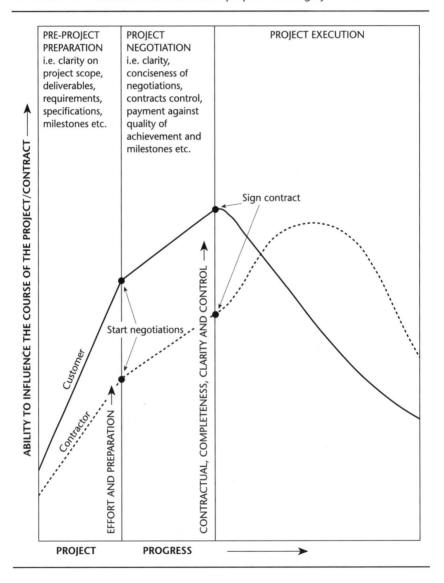

Option 1 is an illustration of this principle.

The customer prepares very thoroughly through basic assessments, pre-feasibility studies and the ultimate feasibility study, so that as much information as is economically feasible is gathered and understood about the product or service envisaged, before the decision is taken to proceed. (See the quality related requirements and deliverables for a project matrix in Chapter 7.)

The contractors that are chosen to tender or negotiate for the contract are competent and experienced in the supply of this, or equivalent types of plants (equipment and service). They have also been briefed, in the information package of the tender documents, on all the salient points that have been learned from the various project feasibility studies.

Under these circumstances, both parties enter negotiations from a stronger, more informed point of view and jointly they can usually negotiate a well-defined, clearly understood contract. It is important to understand that just prior to the signing of the contract, the customer is in his/her strongest position and once it has been signed the 'power of influence' is vested in the contract and the measures and controls it calls up. The customer then substantially loses the ability to influence the project.

The contractor's control of the situation begins to increase as the project progresses and resources are committed for specific hardware and services, while the available time runs its course. During the middle of the project the contractor has the highest ability to influence the course (and consequently costs) of the project with the greatest amount of resources on site at his/her disposal.

As the project progresses and the plant is received, paid for and installed and structures are completed, the contractor's ability to influence the course of the project declines until at the end of the project it is very low. This is because everything is complete and only the final retention monies and areas of dispute have to be resolved. Consequently, his ability to influence the project and its costs only disappears some time after the completion date. This span of time can vary from project to project as certain concessions that were made during the project may influence the cost or quality of product, service or maintenance of the facility for many years to come.

Option 2 illustrates a situation where neither customer nor contractor enter the project well prepared and how disastrous this can be for control and the ability to influence the project and its costs.

In certain instances the contractor loses the ability to influence the project while organizing himself in the beginning. This can cost the

OPTION 2:   Customer and contractor *do not* prepare thoroughly for contract

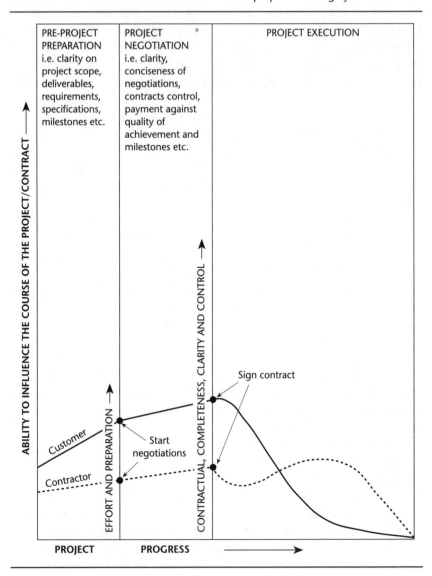

customer very dearly, both with the project and the ultimate plant or facility received. This figure graphically illustrates the importance of thorough preparation prior to commencing a project.

Options 3 and 4 illustrate the various combinations that can be encountered between these extremes.

OPTION 3:   Customer well prepared but contractor poorly prepared for contract

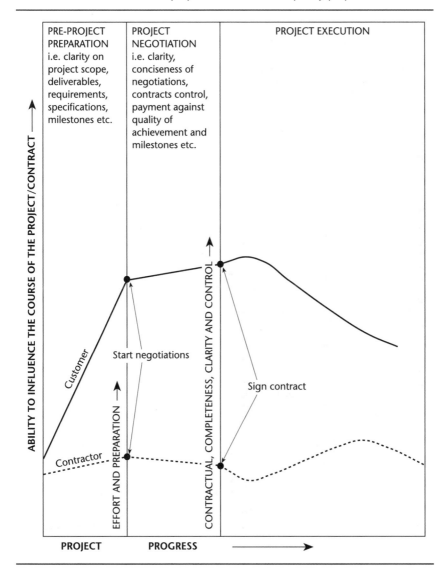

The lesson that experience has taught is that the upfront pre-paredness of both the customer and contractor plays a vital role in the success of the project. Very often both parties rush into a project (especially fast track projects) under the illusion that the preparation can follow, as and when needed. However, the realities of the rapid rate of project progress, cash flow and quality on receipt, never allow this to

OPTION 4: Customer poorly prepared but contractor well prepared for contract

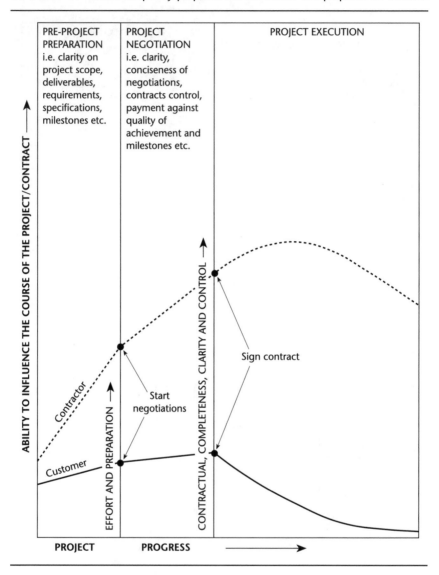

happen to the degree necessary to be able to manage a project professionally. Several of the successful project organizations allow between 20 per cent and 25 per cent of the total project time (including the feasibility study) for the preparation, which ultimately leads to the ability to be able to sign a meaningful contract, allowing proper professional project management.

There are also instances where the correct decision will be to postpone, scale-down or even abort the project altogether, even during the stage of contract negotiation. A decision of this nature at this stage will still be more cost effective than aborting a project after the contract has been signed and work has commenced.

The influence of project budgeting on quality

The influence of cost forecasting on quality

A 'project champion' is often far too optimistic in his/her cost forecast for a project, in order to convince management that their particular project should be given preference. Any project that starts out as a result of understated costs is at a decided disadvantage from the very beginning. This is because this initial estimate often sticks in the minds of management and becomes part of the basis for the decision of management to apportion funds. A cost forecast that is inaccurate, or over-optimistic, will mean that insufficient funds will be allocated and the whole project starts out with the potential of taking short cuts in order to make ends meet.

Kimmons (1990) states that at any stage during the project, the total predicted cost consists of four components:

- the defined elements;

- the contingency;

- the escalation; and

- the job growth.

The cost forecast will have to make allowance for all four of these, although job growth must strictly stay out of the forecast, which should be based on a particular project scope.

There are four quality related aspects that influence cost forecasting or estimating:

- The cost of the quality activities that form an integral part of the defined elements as identified in the work breakdown structure. Failure to identify and cost these thoroughly will ultimately result in insufficient funds in the budget, which will mean that those quality related activities will either not be able to be carried out, or performed only superficially.

- The cost of any corrective action where error or omissions have occurred will also report as a quality cost. These costs will usually have to be funded out of contingency funds.

- The credibility and correctness of the cost estimate should also be reviewed by an objective third party. This is necessary to ensure correctness of assumptions input data, calculations and the overall ultimate estimate. The cost of this review should be allowed for as part of the defined elements, as this should be seen as a legitimate part of the establishment costs.

- Cost of reviewing and correcting the estimates as the process progresses to the point where the estimate can be regarded as definitive because the basic engineering will have been substantially completed.

Kimmons (1990) breaks cost estimating into four phases, namely:

- Viability estimate: This is drawn up from the preliminary scope definition and historical information for the type of facility as scaled up or down. This accuracy is from -25 to $+40$ per cent.

- Appropriation estimate: This is also referred to as a factored estimate, which is based on a more developed scope definition and estimated major equipment costs. The accuracy can vary from -15 to $+25$ per cent.

- Approximate estimate: This makes use of the final scope definition and fairly firm quotations on the major equipment as supplied by prospective suppliers. The accuracy range is from -10 to $+13$ per cent.

- Definitive estimate: This estimate is prepared using material take-offs, quoted equipment and material prices. This is usually carried out after about 40 per cent of the engineering is completed. The accuracy is considered to be from -5 to $+5$ per cent.

Quality and the economic feasibility study

The role of quality is often limited to the market and technical feasibility study only and does not feature in the economic feasibility study.

Oberlender (1993) states that 'regardless of its size or type, a project must be economically feasible'. He also points out that 'for a private project the economic feasibility can be determined by an economic analysis of the monetary return on the investment to build the project.

For a government project the economic feasibility for public projects is usually determined by the benefit/cost ratio.'

Quality plays a role in both instances, as it can both add to and in many instances save on re-work costs. Present experience places quality appraisal and prevention costs in the order of 1.5 to 2 per cent of project costs. A poorly managed and engineered project can incur re-work costs of between 6 and 15 per cent (and even more in certain instances). The calculation of quality costs is discussed in Chapter 7.

It is clear from the abovementioned figures that a 2 per cent cost factor can tip the scales against a marginally economic project. Many projects that were well within economic feasibility have often found themselves floundering because of high costs relating to:

- engineering changes which are made too late and incur structural and equipment changes;

- re-work because statutory safety or process essential quality standards were not met the first time;

- the desired benefits to the customer or stakeholder require higher standards of design, finish, construction or performance before the intended benefit is acceptable to the affected parties.

Oberlender (1993) also states that: 'The economic feasibility can also be influenced by the cost of acceptably disposing of the facility after its useful life'. The payback period method evaluates the number of years 'n' that a project must be operated in order to obtain an interest rate 'i' for a given investment 'P', with an annual generated income of 'A'.

$$P = A \ \frac{(1+i)^n - 1}{i\,(1+i)^n}$$

The cost of acceptably disposing of a facility is also influenced by the final quality of the site after disposal, as several off-shore oil-rig operators have learned to their regret.

The payback period for calculation assumes that the operational quality of the facility can be maintained at an acceptable cost throughout the period calculated. Any rapid unforeseen loss of quality or unexpected maintenance costs will also compromise these calculations. It is therefore necessary that the quality of the facility can be predicted and maintained in a cost effective manner over the desired period of time. Any loss of, or failure to, attain the desired or specified quality standards during construction or establishment will place the entire project in jeopardy for this reason. Oberlender (1993) gives several examples of these calculations, and the reader is referred to his work for more detailed information.

The influence of the project budget on quality

The definitive estimate, together with the contingency estimate, forms the basis of the budget. Kimmons (1990) states that 'the estimate should be broken down according to the work breakdown structure. The budget, however must be expressed in these same WBS terms.'

The final project control budget is the amount of money that the customer agrees to spend on the project for a specified scope of work. The budget should not change unless the scope of work is changed, which should take place in a formal, mutually agreed manner by way of a change order. If the cost of achieving, monitoring and recording the acceptable attainment of customer and stakeholder satisfaction (quality) is not included in the definitive estimates or at worst the contingencies, then these costs will have been 'budgeted out' of the project.

A professional project manager will always reflect quality costs as a clear, separately identifiable item in the budget and obtain approval for these expenditures up front. It is to be expected that the price of not achieving quality which usually reflects in re-work or even scrap costs will have to be balanced by the contingency account. The limited amounts allowed for contingencies also mean that only very limited re-work and scrap costs can be tolerated.

Prevention and appraisal costs are usually less than 10 per cent of correction and scrap costs, and it makes good sense to budget for the prevention and appraisal costs up front, and employ these techniques to best advantage. On many fixed price contracts, money not spent on contingencies reports directly as profits to the managing contractor, or on a 'cost plus' type of contract, reflects as bringing the project in within or under budget. Both of these scenarios are to the benefit of the project management group, and it makes sound financial sense to follow the prevention and appraisal route.

There are many instances where design changes are severe because of a lack of design quality. These changes are major enough to be considered a scope change which will require a budget change. This is a typical instance where the knock-on effect of poor or inadequate quality, as a result of both appraisal and prevention inadequacies of design, only becomes evident later in the project at great expense to the customer and the project management team alike. There have been many instances where a marginally profitable project has had to be aborted because these additional capital costs make the whole venture unfeasible.

The project budget is one of the primary management control instruments which is used to control the flow of resources against the delivery, assembly and erection of acceptable facilities which can be used to ulitmately generate income. An important aspect of the control by management is to ensure that the resources expended do result in a facility that will be profitable to its owner. This is where quality plays a role, in that the payment for completed work must also include acceptably completed milestones in terms of functionally acceptable within design specifications, with all the attendant (not extra) documentation that is necessary. These factors must be included in the work breakdown structure and the contract.

Retention money

The practice of withholding a percentage of the contract price at the end of the project for a specified period of time, in order to have leverage to ensure full and satisfactory completion of the project is widespread. There are also several quality related issues that relate to this final customer satisfaction measure. Full payment should only be made for a fully completed, fully acceptable product or service. Where this does not happen and a part payment is made with the retention of some of the funds in lieu of repair or final completion then certain fundamentals should be considered, namely:

- The value of the retention money should be at least 25 per cent more than the value of the outstanding work or corrective actions to be taken. This will serve as an encouragement to the defaulting party to complete the work. If the retention value is too small there is always a temptation to walk away from the task and accept the loss. The up-front contractual agreement of a retention money formula will motivate a contractor to prevent errors from occurring.

- The use of a flat 10 per cent (or less) as retention money in the contract often leads to problems, especially where severe inadequacies are experienced. It is better to agree on a formula in the contract, whereby the cost of corrective action is established (if necessary by a third party) and a percentage of that cost, say 25 per cent, is added over and above the correction costs.

- The cost of corrective action and the related retention monies should not always be left to the end of a certain package of work. There are cases where major defects occur early in the performance of a task and it may be necessary to stop the work and any progress payments, and fix the problem before proceeding with any further work.

In serious instances of this nature the use of retention money on progress payments can also be of value to ensure the progressive attainment of quality throughout the whole construction or establishment process. This control instrument will have to be negotiated into the project contract from the very beginning and become a contractually acceptable instrument.

It is important to note that as progress payments are made for unacceptable work, the project manager or customer loses any power he/she may have to influence the correction of the problem later. Litigation reflects well on the bottom line of lawyers but seldom on the bottom line of the project. It also almost never adds value once a dispute has arisen. From the abovementioned, it will be evident that the retention money principle does have a very important influence on quality.

The influence of the contractor's bid on quality

The contractor's bid that is accepted for the entire project or a specific part of the project, effectively becomes the budget for that part of the work once it has been accepted and the contract signed. It is therefore necessary to scrutinize the contractor's bid very carefully to make sure that all items, tasks and services required by the scope of work and the work breakdown structure are fully and adequately addressed in the bid before it is accepted.

Oberlender (1993) states that 'Most of the cost of the project is expended during the construction phase when the contractor must supervise large workforces who operate equipment, procure materials, and physically build the project.' It is important from a quality point of view that the quality systems, activities, controls, reporting methods and their attendant (only necessary) documentation be clearly itemized and costed into the bid. Should these be omitted from the bid, or inadequately costed, then all the preceding effort is virtually worthless.

The fundamental here is that what the contactor has bid on in his bid presentation and the customer has accepted is the best the customer can hope for. Any omissions in the bid that the customer accepts are out of the agreed contract, and can only be brought into the contract through a change order with the attendant increase in cost and budget. This principle complements the discussion earlier.

Most activities of the contractor have a quality element in them which must be clearly highlighted and costed. All too often the cost of the quality control and assurance activities and department are the only costs listed in the bid. This is usually sadly inadequate, as the costs are also scattered throughout many other activities such as:

- design review;

- configuration and documentation control. (The same and correct revision of a drawing is supplied to the supplier as well as the site);

- interim inspections on supplied materials, equipment and construction tasks;

- maintenance of product quality in laydown and storage areas;

- maintenance of quality of installed equipment while waiting to be commissioned, i.e. use of special lubricants, rotation of motors – closing of pump, vessel and pipe flanges etc.;

- lightning, rain and other climatic and environmental protection;

- material testing on-site created materials such as welding, concrete and similar activities;

- drafting and acceptance of special procedures and manuals;

- third party inspections;

- interim system testing prior to commissioning;

- cleaning of systems prior to testing;

- costs of special testing teams, equipment and materials;

- cost of drafting special manuals, procedures and quality plans;

- cost of procedure and performance testing and their records and control;

- non-destructive examination of site work, etc.

The applicable list will need to be drafted and reviewed from the work breakdown structure, the work packages and the quality plans in order to arrive at a comprehensive list that can be used to check the contractor's bid. The bid must be very carefully scrutinized by all departments including the quality department, and not only the procurement department, before it is accepted. It is usually necessary to discuss and negotiate such a bid, or preferably list the items that shall also be addressed in the bid and have them separately listed, for ease and accuracy of review before the bid is called for as well as accepted and made contractually binding.

The integration of cost, schedule and quality

Kimmons (1990) states: 'In past years the individual components of the schedule and the budget were not tied to each other. In preparing the schedule and the budget, the two groups went off in different directions.' This is also the experience of the author, with the added problem that at that stage of the process, conventional wisdom dictated that it was too soon to involve quality. The end result was that quality hardly featured in either the schedule or the budget.

The common denominator for the integration of cost, schedule and quality is the work breakdown structure and its work packages and activities, right down to the quality plans where applicable.

It is advisable to carry out these activities by an integrated project team with skilled people in all three disciplines. This integration process should start during the 'approximate estimate' phase and progress through the definitive estimates and ultimately result in an optimized and approved schedule and budget, which includes quality as an integral part.

This process therefore progressively takes into account not only the direct task content in terms of cost and time, but also the quality related attendant activities which also absorb funds and time. The activities listed in the previous section also have to be carefully included in the process, together with other quality related activities that the work breakdown structure and preliminary quality plans may indicate. This integrated management control tool becomes a valuable indicator of successful progress against resources used and the time elapsed as specified by the schedule.

A failure to achieve any one of these three will immediately show up, especially if graphical methods are used to report effective progress. This method, with regards only to physical or system progress, is regarded as complete once all the quality related activities including essential documentation has been completed.

The reporting of acceptable physical progress against time as well as funds committed, invoiced and actually paid, will highlight any deficiencies. In instances where retention money is withheld because of corrections or re-work, the physical progress is reduced by the estimated percentage of outstanding work needed to correct the problem. This gives a better reflection of the value created or earned on the project. This indicator is of value to the customer and stakeholders, and is a clearer reflection of the value for money that they are obtaining.

The use of computers

The computer and cost engineering program have become an essential part of the cost engineering process. Computer programs exist which can help in the development of cost estimates, as well as refine these estimates. There are also programs which will handle most cost management processes and are able to keep management up to date with progress on a daily and, in some instances, an hourly basis. These are very powerful and valuable management tools that have to be evaluated for suitability, user friendliness and value for money.

It is important that software quality assurance be applied to these programs. The factors being used must be relevant and include the applicable quality parameters, otherwise only partial activities will be reported and controlled.

This is a highly specialized field, and when a decision is being taken to use a particular program it is best taken by a representative team rather than a computer expert who may be impressed by the latest technology, rather than taking a holistic view of the overall value to the project.

CASE STUDY

A project champion had developed a new, potentially strategic chemical process that would be marginally profitable if certain cost elements could be removed from the budget.

One of these elements was the purchase of suitable land. It was decided to avoid this cost by using available land already owned by the organization, which was situated some two kilometres away from their present site. The decision was taken not to do any further geophysical surveys but to use the results of the existing site which was 'only' two kilometres away. This would result in considerable cost savings, although it is usually regarded as an essential quality related activity in the ultimate acceptance of a new factory site.

The access road was built and while the site was being fenced for construction, one of the foremen reported discovering a geological sinkhole on the site which needed investigation. The decision was taken to drill only three test holes on a 50 hectare site to confirm acceptability.

The test holes revealed that the 200 metres thickness of unweathered slate had, in the distance of two kilometres, given way to 15 and 20 metres of weathered shale resting on weathered dolomite with serious cavities of 50 and 60 metres across. The whole site was prone to sinkholes, especially in dry periods when the groundwater table would drop and the hydraulic support of the underground caverns would be reduced, giving way to sinkholes.

The whole site and all the fencing and access roads had to be abandoned and a new one obtained, with the attendant losses of time and money. This loss was yet another nail in the coffin of what became an unprofitable project.

CASE STUDY

The cost estimates for fabricating 316L stainless steel pipe spools for a critical class 1 application did not allow for the man hours or materials required to perform a dye penetrant examination of the root run of the weld, as called for in the design specification.

The fabrication of these spools soon fell well behind the over-optimistic schedule and cost overruns were becoming evident. Additional welders were imported and coded for the weld configuration. Two of the new welders appeared to experience no difficulty in meeting the schedule and cost criteria, and almost never had to perform weld repairs on the root run. The schedulers and estimators claimed that this vindicated their estimates and that the other welders were not up to standard.

The welding inspector and foreman who knew the job thoroughly were suspicious and carried out a thorough examination of the process. A routine magnetic test was performed on a completed weld root run. The examination revealed magnetic material and a subsequent metallographic test confirmed that the root run had been carried out using a conventional carbon steel electrode which was much easier and faster to weld.

The welders in question admitted that they had used this technique because the pressures of cost and time had not allowed for the correct procedures to be used. The welders felt that if they added a slight excess of weld bead on the outside it would more than compensate for loss of corroded mild steel in the root run. The deficient welds would have led to the carbon steel root run rapidly corroding because of the acidic process liquids, which would have led to weld and plant failures.

The deficient welds had to be traced from the welding records, the pipe spools removed and the problem corrected. This immediately placed this part of the plant on the critical path and the cost of the repair and time over-run on the late start of production cost the project $US 1.25 million.

Useful tools and techniques

CHAPTER SEVEN

Some useful management tools for quality in projects

Introduction

Management tools are needed to pro-actively ensure and re-actively confirm the key issues for the project's success and the ultimate customer's satisfaction. These tools will vary from project to project, depending upon the nature and technology of the project, as well as its size, complexity and impact.

There are, however, certain management tools that have wide application potential even in the 'one off' nature of a project. It is axiomatic that these tools are generic and will have to be customized to suit the specific conditions and parameters of the project concerned.

Should the reader wish to obtain more detailed information concerning the theoretical basis of these tools or more detailed information for specific applications, then he/she is advised to consult the relevant literature. The references, at the end of this book, will give an indication of some of the applicable literature that is available from the large number of books, videos and computer programs on the subject of quality.

Some prototypal practical examples are given for illustrative reasons and these have been chosen from typical project related activities and could be used with minimum (if any) adaptation. The results of these have been found to be very useful management aids to keep a finger on the pulse of how well things are progressing (quality wise) on the project.

The tools can be broadly divided into those that can be used pro-actively, to help avoid problems, and those that are after the fact, but monitor success and highlight problems. This information can be fed into the system for corrective action and help prevent a continuation and/or proliferation of the problem. There are also tools which can be used as both a pro-active and after the event measure of success.

In instances where the project management group require broader guidance, or a model for assessing how well the whole business is performing, then the reader is referred to a business excellence assessment model.

The two best known models in the sphere are the European Foundation for Quality Management's (EFQM) Business Excellence model and the USA's Malcolm Baldridge Quality Award. Both of these models started out as quality awards and have gradually evolved to a point where the differences between them are not major, and where they currently embrace all the business activities of an organization in a holistic manner.

Many organizations claim that the value in these models lies not with the award only, but with the style of the models and their criteria which give an organization a sound basis for assessing its program towards competitive business excellence.

The use and value of the ISO 9000 Series as a model for quality assurance systems and its related quality manual

The usefulness and value of the ISO 9000 series of quality assurance codes of practice is being recognized by more and more organizations and is currently regarded as the 'quality common denominator' in over 180 countries in the world. These codes of practice (some people refer to them as standards) are not product or project specific, but are generic. They therefore have to be 'customized' for a particular product or project and organization.

This code of practice is increasingly being accepted as a good management tool and a way of managing the production of a product or service, which focuses people's minds on efficient management methods. Its emphasis is on the avoidance of problems and to help show up the weaknesses in the management style, systems and approach. The system is, by implication, aimed at embracing all the major quality influencing activities and personnel in the organization.

It is important to note that ISO 9001 concentrates on the quality of a product or service and not on the business efficiency of an organization. Many people claim that it is not applicable to project work. This, however, is short-sighted as these codes of practice can be applied to any activity that has a defined customer with a need, input, value adding conversion process and output, which must satisfy the needs and expectations of the customer. This therefore automatically includes most projects.

As the name implies, ISO 9000 is not a single document or standard, but consists of a series of documents of which ISO 9000 gives guidance and defines the terms, etc., in order to help the uninitiated. ISO 9004 (part 1) gives guidelines as to the system elements and the correct selection of the appropriate codes. ISO 9001 is the most comprehensive code ranging from design of a product, plant or service, through all the phases of its realization or creation, to the ultimate handover, delivery and despatch (including statistical techniques).

The detailed list of contents can be seen on Table 7.1 (by courtesy of The South African Business of Standards (SABS) and The International Organization for Standardization (ISO)).

The two remaining codes of practice, namely ISO 9002 and 9003, are simplifications of ISO 9001, with ISO 9002 excluding design and 9003 only dealing with final inspection and testing. It is anticipated that at a future date ISO 9002 and ISO 9003 will be dropped as individual codes of practice as they are already included in ISO 9001. Normally a project would use ISO 9001 or ISO 9002. The design group would certainly use ISO 9001, while the sub-contractors who execute the approved design, would generally use ISO 9002.

This code of practice is very valuable when purchasing equipment, materials and services for the project. Specifying the use of organizations with an acceptable ISO 9000 system as the preferred suppliers, where possible, brings a very meaningful standard of management and discipline to the supplier or sub-contractor.

It is important to customize the generic requirements of these codes so that they are project or sub-contractor specific and describe how each organization manages itself for quality (i.e. to do their work correctly) by addressing the system requirements listed in the code of practice.

The management system that results in quality must be thought through and communicated formally so that the document that describes how the organization will manage itself for quality, namely the quality manual (or the management manual for quality) and its supporting procedures and work instructions, can be scrutinized by others.

It is important that this manual and its supporting documents are user friendly so that it is used because it accurately reflects what is happening in the organization with regard to product quality. Many organizations, in former years, used to include the procedures and work instructions in this document as a single all-embracing volume. This resulted in an unwieldy, non-user friendly volume, (or several volumes) consisting of many hundreds of pages, which were difficult to update and therefore often out of date and not used.

TABLE 7.1   The list of contents of ISO 9001 (1994)

Contents		Page
0	Introduction	1
1	Scope and field of application	
	1.1 Scope	1
	1.2 Field of application	1
2	References	1
3	Definitions	1
4	Quality system requirements	2
	4.1 Management responsibility	2
	4.2 Quality system	2
	4.3 Contract review	2
	4.4 Design control	3
	4.5 Document control	3
	4.6 Purchasing	3
	4.7 Purchaser supplied product	4
	4.8 Product identification and traceability	4
	4.9 Process control	4
	4.10 Inspection and testing	4
	4.11 Inspection, measuring and test equipment	5
	4.12 Inspection and test status	6
	4.13 Control of nonconforming product	6
	4.14 Corrective action	6
	4.15 Handling, storage, packaging and delivery	6
	4.16 Quality records	6
	4.17 Internal Quality Audits	7
	4.18 Training	7
	4.19 Servicing	7
	4.20 Statistical techniques	7

Source: The International Organization for Standardization (ISO)

The more modern trend is to keep the procedures separate from the manual and only refer to them in the manual. This results in a management manual for quality that should not be larger than 20–25 pages and preferably between 15 and 20 pages. It can refer to anything between 20 and 50 procedures, possibly supported by as many work instructions, which are stand-alone documents in their own right. These shorter documents should be drafted by the most knowledgeable user, with assistance from a quality profesional, and be a reflection of the actual way of performing tasks. These documents can also be easily updated on an individual basis and remain relevant and useful. The end result is a manual that outlines the management framework for achieving quality that should not take more than 20 minutes to read and which, in turn, is supported by specific procedures and work instructions.

The successful application of the system can be evaluated by using the quality auditing process, a valuable tool for management, giving an indication of the success of the application of their system of management for quality.

The usefulness of the proposed new ISO 10006: A guide to quality in project management

Background information

It is the intention of ISO TC 176 (the technical committee that works with quality management codes of practice and guides) to table the abovementioned guide in order to assist with quality in project management. This document is still in its final draft phase but many of the principles and issues discussed are similar to those used in this book, although terminology and style differ in certain instances.

The guide is in narrative rather than specification form, and most of the issues that are generically discussed in the narrative are covered in a more project specific (yet generic) manner in this book.

The approach to the document

At the time of writing, this ISO document was still in the committee draft (CD) stage. This means that while the document has its basic form, member countries of ISO working on the committee are still free to propose minor changes. At this stage of the document's development these are usually to the detail rather than to the structure or broad principles that have already been set out in the draft in its present form.

It is only after working group consensus by the members participating in drafting the CD has been obtained, that this document can be circulated as a Draft International Standard (DIS) to all the participating ISO member countries for approval. Once this phase has been successfully completed only then can the document be published as an approved ISO standard.

This guideline is intended to provide a structure for the application of quality concepts to the project management process. This document, like many other ISO documents, is intended for a wide range of users, from those experienced in project management and who are applying the quality principles, to those experienced in quality management only and who have to interact with project teams.

The scope of this document as given in ISO/CD 10006 is as follows:

'This guideline gives guidance on those quality principles, practices and quality system elements for which the implementation is important to, and has an impact on, the practice of project management. It is not intended to be a guide to project management itself.

'It gives guidance on the application of quality principles and practices to the management of the processes and activities in the project. It introduces a technique of progress evaluation for monitoring and assessing quality in addition to the status of the project. This guideline is applicable to projects of varying complexity, small or large, of short or long duration, in different environments, and irrespective of the kind of project product including hardware, software, processed material, service or combinations thereof.'

It is important to note that in the definitions section the term 'stakeholder' is defined as: 'Individual or group of individuals with a common interest in the performance of the supplier organization and the environment in which it operates.'

This consideration of the interests of stakeholders as well as customers is relatively new, and coincides with the author's experience that this is becoming an aspect of project management that will require increased attention by management. Reference to the matrix in the last chapter will illustrate to the reader practical ways as to how this can be addressed. There are those in this committee who even feel that customers are a subset of the stakeholder concept. This document concentrates on the aspects that the project management team must give attention to in order to achieve quality (customer and stakeholder satisfaction) during and on completion of the project, as well as the operation of the facility it has established.

It is important to note that attention is not only given to the quality of the end product but also to the process of project management as a means to achieve the desired end result. The process approach is used because it does not get 'bogged down' in the various phases of a project but concentrates on the activities required to meet the project's objectives.

However, in active project management the project manager cannot avoid the typical phases of a project. This does however give him/her a tool that can be used during any phase of the project. This document lists the project management processes which can be used during the planning and execution of any project in Table 1 of its annexure. The basic structure of project management processes is shown in Figure 1 of the guideline.

There are three major inputs into the project management processes for quality, namely:

- those of the customer;

- the identification of the stakeholders (which includes the customers) and their needs that the project must satisfy, or at least not violate;

- the input of the ISO 9000 requirements as a standard for quality management.

The operational aspects of the project management process are broken down into eight aspects, all of which are co-ordinated by one of the major aspects of any management process – namely, communication and integration.

The eight sub-sets in this process are the following:

- strategy;

- scope;

- product evaluation (this includes services);

- procurement;

- risk;

- resources;

- personnel;

- cost;

- time;

- communication.

The question that automatically arises is that of the apparent absence of quality. A revisit to our explanation of quality, namely the satisfaction of customers' and stakeholders' needs, will show that customers' and/or stakeholders' needs have to be met progressively by each of these activities.

In order to achieve customer and stakeholder satisfaction, quality must be a major product of good management, and therefore one of the major outputs of the project management process. The reader is referred to Chapter 2 on the universal process model (and nature) of all processes. All of the activities listed in this operational process model are both individually and collectively aimed at meeting a particular need of a customer and/or stakeholder, in other words a successful project.

Project characteristics and project management

This is further discussed in section 4 of ISO/CD 10006 *Guideline to Quality in Project Management* (1995), International Organization for Standardization.

Through time mankind has had various needs, some relatively straightforward that the individual can solve either alone or with the aid of existing infrastructure and skills. There are, however, many occasions when the need is of such a nature that special resources and skills have to be assembled to establish a system and/or infrastructure of greater complexity in order to meet this need, within an acceptable period of time, and within budget. These resources have to be managed in an optimal manner to ensure that the objectives and scope of this project are met. All projects have an element of uniqueness about them, but there are many routine activities that also have to be carried out in order to achieve the desired end result.

The document explains that 'Project management includes the planning, organizing, monitoring and controlling of all aspects of the project in a continuous process to achieve its project objectives, both external and internal. It is a discipline requiring the application of skills, tools and techniques and the balancing of competing demands of product specification, time and cost.'

'Project management incorporates the quality management function.'

'The quality of the project management process has a significant effect on the success of a project and on the quality of the project outputs.'

'The project manager is the individual appointed with the responsibility and authority for managing the project. The authority delegated to the project manager should be commensurate with the responsibility.' This title may vary from project to project.

The success of a project depends not only on the quality of the end product, but also on the project management process. It is interesting to note that the trade-off concepts listed do not include volume and the environment, as both have an influence on a project and in many instances projects influence the environment. In the author's opinion it is necessary to take these into account as well in the whole process of managing projects in order to achieve quality.

This document also considers the phases of a project which broadly concur with those discussed in the last three chapters of this book. The detail given in the last three chapters is far greater than that discussed during the deliberation on these guidelines.

The process approach of these guideline recognizes the sequence of the phases in any project. The process approach was selected 'because it relates directly to the activities, required to meet project objectives and avoids the complications inherent in dealing with its phases. The process approach cuts across the boundaries between phases.' The guidelines in the document and this book are therefore complementary and help to give the reader a more holistic view of the quality aspect of the total project management process.

Fundamental quality principles

This important and informative section is discussed in section 5 of *Guideline to Quality in Project Management*, and gives an overview of the fundamental principles that influence quality and which must be included in the whole project management strategy and process.

The principles listed are the following:

'Principle 1: Maximizes the satisfaction of customers' and other stakeholders' needs; is paramount.

Principle 2: All work on a project is carried out as a set of planned and interlinked processes.

Principle 3: Quality has to be built into both product and processes.

Principle 4: Management is responsible for creating an environment for quality.

Principle 5: Management is responsible for continuous improvement.'

The author supports these principles strongly. The customer is the reason for the existence of the project, and special attention should be given to this fact. The concept of legitimate needs is important as the satisfaction of the customer's needs cannot be at the expense of others, or the environment. The reader is also referred to the holistic project management process as discussed in Chapter 2.

Quality in project operations (section 6 of Guideline to Quality in Project Management)

This guideline reviews quality in project operations which provides guidance on the application of quality practices that cascade from the five quality principles for projects. The various processes are arranged into a hierarchy, which are related to their functional objectives.

This hierarchy follows the natural progression usually followed in more conventional management processes. The processes listed below can all be found in *Guideline to Quality in Project Management*.

- strategic processes (section 6.2);

- interlinking processes (section 6.3);

- scope related processes (section 6.4);

- time related processes (section 6.5);

- cost related processes (section 6.6);

- resource related processes (section 6.7);

- personnel related processes (section 6.8);

- communication related processes (section 6.9);

- risk related processes (section 6.10);

- procurement related processes (section 6.11).

These are expanded upon in Table 1 of the same book's Annexure 'D' which can be used as a checklist for management in order to ensure that all the various applicable management processes are addressed. Explanations are given of what should be taken into consideration in all of the subsections of the process list. These, although they are generic, do give management very valuable tools to use.

It is important to note that this guideline is not intended to be a detailed project management textbook but a guideline to the aspects that will need attention in order to achieve quality in the project.

The discussions of the requirements that are listed in the subsections listed above make up the bulk of the document.

There is also an Annexure 'B' which cross-references the clauses of ISO 10006 to those of ISO 9001 as well as ISO 9004-1. This is a very useful table which makes it easier for the reader to find his or her way around the related documents.

The use of quality auditing techniques

Quality auditing has many parallels with financial auditing in as much as it is a process that is used by trained and skilled people who objectively examine a system, process and end results in order to evaluate its credibility and application against set criteria.

A quality auditor will study the formal process that was designed by the responsible management, in order to be sure that a desired end result has the maximum chance for repeated success, as well as providing a product or service that conforms to the requirements of the deliverables needed to satisfy the customer's needs. The first is often referred to as a systems audit, while the second is referred to as a product audit.

An audit is essentially a 'statistical snapshot' of what can be demonstrated to be happening for the reviewing third party (the auditor) in comparison with what management planned should happen. Management's plans and commitment to consistently achieve a desired result (quality) are usually documented in the quality manual and its supporting quality plans, procedures and work instructions. Most of the key processes are fields of specialization in their own right and there is a substantial amount of published literature that covers the successful management of these issues.

The management for quality (of each of these issues), in terms of sound quality principles, is an improvement or refinement of these disciplines and should not be seen as the creation of a whole new discipline. These topics focus more on the process of managing for quality, rather than the achievement of the end result or required deliverable. If this management process occurs successfully the quality of the deliverable should follow automatically.

The author wishes to warn that in the older approach to project quality, there was a tendency to follow the conformance to specification route only. A great deal of emphasis was placed on defining the quality of the deliverable with only scant or, at best, patchy attention being given to the process whereby the desired end result would be obtained. It is essential that both aspects should receive their correct amount of attention, i.e. both the process as well as the end result.

The quality auditor will review both these and compare them to the standard (or norm), usually ISO 9001 or 9002, called up in the quality manual, and assess whether the typical minimum elements required for success have been adequately addressed.

During this study he/she will draw up a checklist of specific important areas in the system and when this has been completed, he/she will check, in practice, whether these actions are being carried out in a responsible, regular, formal (documented) manner, so as to gain confidence that these key activities are happening, are under control and where necessary are traceable.

This process is usually expanded to include the relevant product or service to ensure that the system that is being applied ultimately gives the desired product or service that the customer wants.

If a quality audit is to be credible it must also happen in a formal and auditable manner as well. There are certain formalities that enhance and ensure an audit's credibility, namely:

- It is carried out by suitable, trained and approved people.

- Formal arrangements exist for the audit and its scope acceptance.

- Formal obtaining of applicable documentation.

- An agreed audit scope, date, schedule and requirements in terms of people and facilities.

- A formal audit opening meeting, agenda attendance record and minutes, where applicable.

- As the audit progresses, the auditors are accompanied by the relevant management representative/s.

- Auditors are allowed reasonable access to the areas under review.

- Any problems found (observations or findings) are discussed at the place of the incident or observation with the auditee's representative and mutually (usually formally) agreed that it was actually observed.

- A formal audit close-out meeting in which the audit, its success and any 'observations' (quality influencing incident) or 'findings' (more serious problems that will compromise quality) are presented, discussed, and modified (if necessary) and a final audit report agreed upon.

- The audit report is formally responded to by the auditee and a commitment is made to correct problems.

- Follow up audits or assessments are carried out in order to assess the extent and success of the agreed corrective action.

This process is a valuable management tool in order to get a 'non-filtered', impartial view of events or activities affecting quality and management success during the course of the project.

Quality audits can be very broad or very focused depending upon the circumstances and the need. They can be internal and be carried out by the organization's own quality auditors who examine the organization's own system and practices for quality. The auditing process may also examine an outside organization or sub-contractor to establish their potential to achieve quality of goods or services supplied. This provides management with an assessment as to whether they are suitable for, or actually achieving the desired end results of the project. An external or third-party audit can also be done when the customer or management contracts a professional quality auditing company to perform an independent quality audit on the organization.

Training

Quality is usually achieved directly or indirectly by and through people, and the role of the people in quality must never be underestimated. The training and skills needed on a project are often formulated in an 'ad hoc' manner and built into the job description, very often by people (often personnel or senior management) who are not familiar with the detailed skills required to perform the task.

One of the best places to address the qualifications, training and skills required to perform a task is at the very basis of task description and definition, namely the work procedure or instruction. It is advisable to let the appropriate, skilled, operating or trade people, who basically draft the procedures or work instruction, include a section which sets out the qualifications and skills required to ensure that the person who has to carry out the procedure or work instruction is skilled enough to be able to perform the task or function repeatedly with success.

Any task will, therefore, require certain basic abilities as well as specific training and skills for it to be performed satisfactorily. This can expand to include several procedures and work instructions that cover the special activities of a specific type of task. The total education, skills and training required is the sum of these in order for the incumbent to be able to perform quality work (perform successfully). Skills in this context are regarded as practised training and procedures to the point of self confidence where errors are unlikely to occur. Project management must take cognizance of these and build the necessary training needs and resources into their planning to ensure that the correct people are employed and/or trained for the project, to the desired level of skill.

Non-destructive examination (NDE)

This is a process that is carried out in order to examine materials, components or assemblies for flaws, physical properties or in some instances, typical chemical properties, without affecting or substantially impairing the ability of the item examined to perform its function (provided that it is acceptable).

There are many good books which cover the various techniques in detail and the reader who requires more information would be advised to consult them. The American Society for Testing and Materials (ASTM) has many standards on non-destructive testing, and the reader is advised to refer to them.

It is important to understand that NDE can only be carried out by people who have been trained and, through experience, have acquired the necessary skills to conduct the particular examinations properly and interpret the results professionally.

NDE is usually contracted out to specialist contracting companies that have been accredited and have staff qualified and certified in the specific field of NDE to be used. These techniques in the hands of unskilled people can be both dangerous, in terms of not detecting unacceptable errors, and costly because they can have an acceptable (or even non-existent) defect removed and repaired unnecessarily or, worse still, have an acceptable component scrapped.

This form of examination occurs after the event of creating the component or performing the task and can do very little for the quality of the item under question in terms of preventing the nonconformity. It can, however, facilitate the decision of whether to repair or not. Selective use of NDE during the creation of a component, e.g. a key activity such as the root run of a weld, can prevent the performance of work on an already unacceptable item. It is valuable in preventing the use of defective items, or further processing of faulty ones only to be found unacceptable later, or, even worse, fail in service. It does, therefore, give confidence that the various processes are operating successfully and under control.

The NDE process generates a substantial amount of data and, if correctly used, this data can be processed and analysed to give valuable operating management information, which can be used to identify areas of a process or even operators (especially in welding) that do not have the capability of repeatedly giving a reliable product or service. This information can be used to identify the problem and its root cause and thus help to eliminate it.

Where statutory equipment is being manufactured, installed or repaired, most engineering codes require NDE in order to give assurance that the end product is safe and fit for use. NDE results can also be used in trend analysis whereby a slow shift in process results can be detected at an early stage and corrected before errors occur. This form of examination can also be used to keep 'the finger on the pulse' of operator performance in operator critical processes such as welding or casting. Welders or foundrymen that have lost their touch or who may need more training because they do not have the desired consistency of acceptable results can also be highlighted.

CASE STUDY:

In one problematic aluminium welding process of a particular project, each welder had to produce three X-ray and vacuum test acceptable welds before the welder was allowed to continue with production. If he was unable to do so after the sixth attempt he would be rested for the day, with a loss of production bonus. This was to ensure that short term skill problems did not negatively affect the high standard of workmanship that was needed for success. Within eight weeks weld defects fell to less than 1 per cent of welds performed.

Table 7.2 is a list of some of the more generally acceptable NDE methods that are used on projects.

TABLE 7.2 Generally acceptable NDE methods used on projects

Type	Use	Advantages	Disadvantages
Dye penetrant	Detects cracks that are open to the surface. Application is straightforward by means of aerosol.	Quick, accurate and simple to apply. Can be used in places that are difficult to access and also on almost any material.	Surfaces must be clean. Surface grinding can affect results. Defects must reach the surface.
Magnetic particle test	Detects surface flaws as well as those that are sub-surface, yet close enough to affect the magnetic field.	A simple method that gives almost immediate indication. Can detect defects that do not break to the surface. Flexibility.	Only works on ferro-magnetic metals (iron, steel). Cracks parallel to magnetic field not detected. Tests at right angles also needed. Surfaces must be clean.
X-ray	Detects internal defects such as cracks, slag and other inclusions. Can be used on a variety of materials if correct ray parameters are used. Suitable for testing welds.	Shows flaws below the surface for relatively thick material up to 100mm steel and more. Indicates nature of flaw, gives a permanent record in the file (film). Source of radiation can be switched off electrically.	Fairly high initial cost. Radiation hazard. Insensitive if defect size less than 2% of wall. Needs trained operators. Equipment is usually heavy. Affected by non-uniform materials.
Gamma ray	Similar to X-ray. Can be used to check variations in thickness of material. Suitable for tests on weld integrity.	Same as for X-rays. Needs no or limited electrical power. Lower initial cost than X-ray. Can penetrate thick materials more easily.	Irradiation intensity fixed. Correct isotope must be chosen for use. Trained technicians needed. Source decays in strength. Not as sensitive as X-rays. Results have to be processed. Needs trained operators.

TABLE 7.2 *Continued*

Type	Use	Advantages	Disadvantages
Eddy current	Tests for wall thickness variation and material properties. Tests thickness of coating and surface irregularities. Checks pipe integrity as well as paint quality.	High speed non-contact testing. High sensitivity suitable for detecting small pin holes. Can operate in conditions of poor visibility.	Can only be used on electrically conductive materials. Comparative measurements possible. Methods not absolute. Affected by temperature and magnetic fields.
Ultrasonic test	Tests for wall thickness variation, internal cracks, noise and porosity	Flexible between internal defects down to porosity not dependent on flaws	Cannot reach all areas. Needs a lubricant contact. Needs highly skilled operator.

Source: Reproduced with kind permission of McGraw Hill Book Company and based on Table 1847 of Juran's *Quality Control Handbook* (1988)

The use of statistical quality control (SQC) techniques

The application of statistical techniques for measuring and improving the quality of processes on projects is becoming more commonplace. SQC includes statistical process control, diagnostic tools, sampling plans and other statistical methods. The reader is referred to section 24 of *Juran's Quality Control Handbook* (1988), McGraw Hill, for further detail.

The underlying role is to gather data concerning the performance or features of a process operation or product/service, and to study or analyse it to be able to decide whether a lot is acceptable or whether the process is operating under control. This information can also be used to improve processes and give early warning when things are starting to go wrong, so that errors can be corrected or prevented.

Usually statistical process control requires drawing a sample from a process or a lot that is producing a significant number of items or results.

Many people feel that this is not applicable to projects which are usually 'one off' by nature. However, this is not true as within most projects there are many tasks which are of a repetitive nature and which are suitable for statistical process control in order to ensure that the operation is functioning stably and under control.

Statistical process control can therefore typically be applied to controlling the following project activities:

- concrete mixing (or purchase);

- site-run welds;

- soil compaction;

- painting and quality of painted surfaces;

- termination of cabling;

- supply of bulk materials;

- analysis of variation orders;

- design queries;

- analysis of design changes.

There are many other activities on a project that can benefit from these techniques. The design and implementation of the correct statistical method requires the skills of suitably trained applied statisticians, but the procedure and its parameters have been incorporated into codes, etc., and so designed that they can usually be used by semi-skilled people with success, and are therefore a valuable tool to management and operators alike.

Some of the more well-known forms of statistical methods are the following:

Sampling inspection – By random or variable methods.

Pareto diagrams – To determine the significant few parameters that have the greatest influence.

Control charts – To establish the random and assignable causes of variation to directly monitor the stability, predictability and capability of a process.

Pre-control limits – The dividing of the tolerance into three zones. The required tolerance zone is bounded by the warning zone that indicates unwanted change. This empowers the worker to leave the process alone, or make corrections as needed.

The use of averages	–	To give an indication of the position of the whole 'population' under consideration.
The use of operating characteristic curve	–	To understand the distribution characteristic of the process.
Trend analysis	–	Plotting the trends of the results to obtain an indication as to where the process is going (or changing to).

This section is intended to give an insight into some of the techniques available to management. These techniques allow management to gain an insight into how well the repetitive processes on the project are under control, and to allow them to take timeous corrective action where and when it is needed. This subject is also covered by several textbooks.

Statistical processes, in the hands of unskilled and inexperienced people, can be very misleading and lead to incorrect management decisions, and it is important that the procedures and criteria are designed by suitably skilled persons.

The use of quality plans

The quality plan, in its simplest form, is a list of all the individual activities that are identified in the work breakdown structure of an individual task. Each activity is listed along with the requirements and specifications that govern the successful completion of the activity.

These requirements and specifications are supported by the procedures and/or work instructions that describe the activity (where necessary).

The integration of these into one list or plan gives all the activities as well as the essence of the quality aspects that govern the activity, which, if all are correctly carried out, will lead to an acceptable task. It is, however, of value to add additional information to this basic plan to make it more useful as a project management tool.

If a critical activity is included in a quality plan and it is vital that this activity or the sum of the preceding activities is correct, then a 'hold point' can be indicated on the plan. This is a point beyond which work may not proceed until the activity has been inspected, tested or monitored by a designated inspector or authority and approved. It is also quite common, where the activity is important but not critical, that a 'witness' point is indicated in the plan. Usually this is where the foreman, client or third party would like to be notified that this stage has been reached and that they are free to inspect or observe the activity. This step is optional and may be taken up or waived by the customer or inspecting authority or representative.

Many quality plans also have the required inspections and even the inspection documentation required, indicated on them. As the activity progresses, a data file of inspection reports, NDE results, material certificates, etc. as indicated by the quality plan is progressively built up as completion of the specific tasks that make up the activity progresses. Very often a task can be inspected and signed off by the person performing it as a first indication of its successful completion. This may also be followed up by a foreman's or inspector's signature on the quality plan indicating successful completion and inspection or test.

A large or complex activity may have a generic quality plan at the broad work breakdown level. This plan can be supported by many other quality plans detailing the planning for quality of the various sub-activities and their tasks.

Quality plans should be drawn up by the management and staff who are actually going to perform the task, as they are directly responsible for the quality of the work that they perform. The managing contractor or customer should never fall into the trap of drafting quality plans for sub-contractors for several reasons, namely:

- If the sub-contractor cannot draft their own quality plans, they are usually not competent enough to do the work properly (especially if it is of a more complex nature).

- The sub-contractor is seldom committed to make somebody else's plan work for them.

- It gives the sub-contractor somebody to blame when the work is not acceptable.

- The customer or managing contractor is not fully aware of the sub-contractor's procedures, skills and equipment and can easily draft a plan that the sub-contractor cannot follow.

The managing contractor's or the customer's quality department and project engineer (or both) should review the quality plans submitted to them so that they can ascertain the readiness level of the sub-contractor and the amount of planning and effort that has gone into preparing for the task.

This review and acceptance (or otherwise) also allows the managing contractor or customer to indicate his/her hold and witness point requirements as well as the amount of additional supporting documentation that he/she may require. Many small projects are often only run on quality plans and not with a specific project quality manual. The contractor's general quality manual supported by quality plans is often sufficient.

Quality costing

Basic approach to costing

Money is the common language of management and it is sensible to measure, analyse and communicate the success of the quality system and its functioning in the language of money.

Dr Barrie Dale in *Managing Quality* (1994) states that 'Quality cost may be regarded as a criterion of quality performance – but only if valid comparisons can be made between different sets of cost data.'

Professor Gryna in section 4 of *Juran's Quality Control Handbook* (1983) uses quality costs as meaning the cost of poor quality. Feigenbaum (1996) helped to entrench the prevention–appraisal–failure categorization of quality costs. Crosby's (1979) philosophy is to divide quality costs into the cost of conformance and the cost of non-conformance.

Project management can use either the first or the second categorization for quality costs. The author, however, feels that the use of the prevention/failure categorization is more suited to project management than the cost of conformance/cost of non-conformance approach.

The discussion in the preceding chapter has emphasized that quality must be approached holistically. This is also applicable to the categorization collection and reporting of the cost relating to quality.

Most of the project activities and phases have initial activities in which considerable effort is expended in making sure that the most applicable information, project scope, planning, cost estimates etc. are gathered. This is done in an effort (because of the general one off nature of projects) to prevent things from going wrong in the first place. Progressive reviews of activities for completeness and correctness are also carried out as an ongoing appraisal of the acceptability of progress.

Corrective action is also necessary from time to time to make sure that an acceptable project is ultimately handed over to the customer. The cost of this corrective action due to a failure to meet specifications can usually be established and quantified in terms of money and therefore a quality or non-quality cost on most projects.

Cost gathering responsibilities

The success of the quality costing system is heavily dependent on how well it is integrated into the rest of the project management systems. The quality cost gathering system must not be seen as an optional add-on, but rather as an integral part of the total cost gathering system and must be an integral part of the cost engineering activity.

The cost engineering department, together with the quality department, will have to form a team and jointly with the other activities of the project define what the quality activity elements of that function are, and fit them in with existing cost structures which will normally flow out of the work breakdown structure. These cost elements should be clearly defined in user-friendly terms so that 'non quality staff' such as accountants and cost engineers can work with them comfortably.

CASE STUDY:

Examples:

- In the design function effort is expended in double checking input information. This error check function in terms of cost of man hours and cost of obtaining corroborating information can be regarded as a prevention quality cost for design.

- The cost of a design review or a third party statutory review of the design can be regarded as a design appraisal quality cost.

- The cost of making corrections to a design in terms of cost of design man hours and, where applicable, materials as well as cost of re-work as a result of the design error right through to the correction of the documentation, can all be regarded as design failure costs.

The sum of these three costs represents some of the major costs of quality for design.

It is also important to define where the cut off points of a cost element are, and what constitutes a quality cost and what is the normal cost of the activity. For example, if there has been a problem with design and the problem has only surfaced during the use of the design to fabricate, install or erect an item, should the cost of re-work also be added on to the failure cost of design or not? If in the opinion of the design and construction management teams it was an avoidable error, then the cost of re-work of the item or system that was under construction should be added to the design failure cost as an integral part thereof. If the error was a result of an unforeseeable issue then the re-work cost should still be reported under design failure cost but identified as unforeseeable, or unavoidable cost.

The purpose of identifying quality costs

The purpose of identifying and reporting on these costs is in order to facilitate the achievement of the following:

- To highlight the importance of the holistic quality approach and functions to the full project management team.

- To encourage individuals and teams to take responsibility for the quality of the work they perform.

- To make comparisons of performance between projects.

- To help to obtain more accurate cost estimates and budgets for future projects.

- To provide cost information for motivational or management action purposes.

- To highlight problem areas in the project that may need special attention.

- To assist with vendor rating which can be categorized as follows:

- The need for and cost of receiving inspection of items from a supplier.

- Quantification of supplier product costs.

- Source inspection cost.

- Purchased material replacement cost.

- Supplier caused reject and scrap costs.

The collection of costs

The cost engineering department should be involved from the very beginning. Dale (1994) states that 'The methodology adopted by an organization for the collection of costs must be practical and relevant in that it contributes to the performance of the basic activities of the organization.' The list of cost elements included in BS 6143 part 2 (1990) can be considered but will have to be customized in order to make them more project specific. Ultimately the total collection list will also have to be based on the experience of the project management team.

Inspection and testing

What is inspection and testing?

Inspection in this text means reviewing and evaluating the conformance of an achieved characteristic against a standard or specification. Testing is also a form of evaluation, but in this text means assessing the acceptability of functionality against a standard or specification.

Zeccardi in Section 18 of *Juran's Quality Control Handbook* (1988) states that the 'inspection act' consists of the following actions applied to each quality characteristic:

- interpretation of the specification;

- measurement of the quality of the characteristic;

- comparison of the two above points;

- judging conformance;

- disposing of conforming cases;

- disposing of non-conforming cases;

- recording the data obtained.

The author would like to add an eighth item analysing the data for trends in order to convert the data into management information that can be used for continous imporvement.

Zeccardi, in *Juran's Quality Control Handbook*, 4th Edition (1988) expands on the term, measurement, as it is used in the generic sense of evaluation as follows:

When the measurement is done by the unaided human being	The word commonly used to describe it is inspection (the author also uses visual inspection)
With the aid of mechanical measuring instruments	Gauging or callipering (the author also uses the term measurement inspection)
With the aid of electronic measuring instruments	Testing
With the aid of chemical or metallurgical measuring instruments	Testing or assaying. (The author also uses the terms chemical or metallurgical analysis)

Table 18.1 of *Juran's Quality Control Handbook* (1988) further lists the purposes of inspection in terms of what the purpose is, what the activity is usually called, and what the distinguishing features are. From this it follows that the people who perform inspection must be fully conversant and skilled in the technology of the item that they inspect, otherwise they will not be able to judge conformance effectively. An inspector must also be skilled and preferably certified in the measurement techniques required to measure the quality of the characteristics.

Many organizations employ older and more mature tradesmen and technicians who have been involved with the technology for many years as inspectors. Such an individual will need training in the technique and process of inspection but it does imply that they have the maturity and credibility to make sound judgement and successfully interpret specifications.

As technology progresses so do the requirements for inspection personnel increase. Many high technology activities require the services of highly trained and often graduate staff as inspectors. Inspection is therefore not a cheap activity or process and, important as it is, it has to be used circumspectly, as it is also part of the cost chain and in its own way must add value to the product or system.

Inspection is usually an after the fact activity, and gives confidence on conformance but does little to prevent things from going wrong on the already completed item. The information can be used to help prevent errors on other similar items or systems that still have to be made, designed or installed.

How much inspection?

There is a misconception amongst some people in projects that 'multiple layers of inspection' lead to better quality. This is not true; in fact often quite the reverse is true.

CASE STUDY:

The author, while reviewing the material certificates of a special grade of stainless steel for a special pressure vessel in the chemical industry, was surprised to note that the percentages of alloying elements quoted were for a different alloy. The relevant specifications were consulted and the author's initial observations were found to be correct. The material had been manufactured by a very reputable stainless steel manufacturer in the United Kingdom. The material certificate had been reviewed and bore the signatures of that organization's smelt house foreman, chief chemist, works metallurgist, as well as that of the third party inspectorate responsible for the vessel and the chief inspector of the vessel fabrication company. In all there were five layers of inspection and only the sixth one, myself, spotted the error. The material had to be replaced with all the attendant delays and cost. The author calls this 'multiple inspection syndrome'.

The author's experience is that where there is multiple inspection, many of the initial inspectors rely on the fact that if they miss anything the subsequent inspections will pick it up. On the other hand the subsequent inspectors feel that the first inspector would have picked up any errors and reported on them and is therefore more lax with the inspection. The responsible inspector must know that he/she is finally responsible for the success (quality) of the inspection and be fully diligent from the outset.

The answer to the question of how much inspection has two facets, namely:

- A clear contractual understanding of who is responsible for compliance with specifications.

- How critical is the item or system.

Responsibility for quality and inspection

The following should be clearly understood and as far as possible it should be contractually specified that:

■   The individual or team performing the work is responsible for its quality, i.e. getting the task right first time and every time.

■   The management and supervision of the organization that contracted to perform the work are responsible for reviewing and assessing that the specifications have been fully met, such as:

   ■   The vendor is responsible for the quality of the product or system that they supply.

   ■   The subcontractor is responsible for the quality of the subcontracted work.

   ■   The managing or general contractor is responsible for the quality of work that they have contracted to perform.

   ■   The owner's management team have an ultimate responsibility to their senior management and where applicable, stakeholders (including shareholders).

The inspection team should never be used as the 'primary filter' for mistakes but rather to finally assess that all the requirements of the specification have been fully met.

Testing is one of the forms of inspection to demonstrate the achievement of acceptable functionality. Third party or independent inspection is usually employed on safety or operationally critical items or systems where for safety or statutory reasons an independent review is needed. Inspectors performing this type of work are trained in these techniques and usually do not fall into multiple inspection syndrome! They are trained to carefully review work that has already been inspected and accepted for latent errors or oversights that could lead to future problems.

The influence of criticality in inspection levels

The amount of inspection needed can also be influenced by the criticality of the component or system or even the criticality of a limited number of parameters within the system. Safety critical items are usually covered by statutory requirements, and the use of a third party independent inspectorate is mandatory.

It is the responsibility of the designer to highlight whether statutory inspections are called for or not. The designer should also classify the non-statutory governed items according to whether they are critical or not. He/she should, where applicable, also specify the amount of inspection needed to ensure that the design intent that has been communicated in the drawings, specification and other documents has been achieved, by calling for specific inspections and test procedures. A competent designer should also indicate which of the parameters of the design are functionally critical and whether they are major or minor, so that the amount and level of inspection and test can be determined.

This form of seriousness classification needs to be done as a team effort between the design and the manufacturing and inspection teams so that an optimum and cost effective inspection and test programme can be formulated, specified and planned.

The criticality of items or parameters flows from this specification exercise so that both the manufacturer or erector and the inspection department can place the effort and resources where they will be effective and add the most value. The reader is referred to tables 18.9 and 18.10 in *Juran's Quality Control Handbook* (1988) for examples of how this can be achieved.

Planning and organizing inspection and testing

There are five major areas to be considered when planning inspection and testing on projects, namely:

- the establishment of inspection levels based on the criticality of parameter and component levels;

- the acceptance of procured items and materials;

- the acceptance of site fabricated items;

- field inspection and test;

- preservation of quality during storage as well as after instalment before commissioning.

Planning as a function of criticality of parameters and components

Planning of inspection really starts with the design – manufacturing – quality group during the classification of the criticality of functions and defects during the design stage. This is because the planning of the inspection activities must also be done by people who have a thorough knowledge of the use and fitness for use factors of a system or item, i.e. the designer. This must also be supported by those who have to convert the design into a functional system item or service, because they will have the best insight as to where things can go wrong during the manufacturing or fabrication process.

In many instances it is only the inspection team who will have enough knowledge of the limitations of their special processes to be able to optimally use interim inspections and reviews, because subsequent operations may make inspection difficult or impossible at a later stage. From this discussion it will be evident that not all inspection or testing activities should or need to be done by the inspection or quality control department. Many inspections (especially those of an interim nature) can and should be done by the competent technical staff who actually do the work.

The quality plan should be the output of these tri-party planning discussions as this is the basic planning and organizing specification agreed upon by the designer, the performer of the work and the quality team. The quality plan should become an integral aspect of the total job planning process and should play a significant role in the selection of fabrication methods. This is important because adequate process reliability and control is needed to meet the needs of critical parameters and components. Only after this has been completed can the resources required for in process and acceptance inspection be planned and deployed.

The acceptance of procured items

The fundamental principle that applies to procured items is that the supplier is responsible for assuring and demonstrating conformance to requirements to the satisfaction of the customer's or main contractor's inspection team.

The requirements of inspection testing and documentation have to be included in the procurement contract and be contractually binding if inspection and testing is to happen properly. The information of critical, major and minor parameters and items must also be conveyed to the suppliers or manufacturer of the design.

In instances where the designer calls for standard off the shelf items then all catalogue specified test results and reports need to be received and accepted prior to final acceptance inspection by the customer.

When items have to be manufactured or fabricated it is advisable to call for a quality plan from the supplier so that his inspection input can be reviewed. It is only after this review that the customer or main contractor can decide whether or not they wish to establish hold points in the quality plan based upon the requirements of the design. This will also give the client's inspection group an indication of how much, if any, acceptance inspection has to be performed in the suppliers' presence.

The final acceptance inspection can only be carried out on the component once it has been delivered to the main contractors' site store where the responsibility of ownership passes from the supplier to the main contractor or customer. The final acceptance inspection is important to verify that there has been no damage to the item or other loss of quality in transit.

The acceptance of site fabricated items

The principle that the site fabrication team is responsible for the quality of their work still applies.

A site fabrication system must be treated in basically the same manner as that of an external supplier as discussed earlier. Once again the principle of establishing a quality plan is applicable. The very first inspection for acceptability should be carried out by the person performing the work, who should be operating in a state of self control.

The next line of review for acceptability (inspection) should be the responsible foreman. Only after this should the inspector be involved, and then only as required by the quality plan. Many construction sites use the available inspection staff of the quality department to carry out inspections of site fabricated items directly. This often makes good management sense and avoids the duplication of the inspection activities, as well as being more cost effective, but must be used judiciously.

Field inspection and testing

Kimmons in his book on *Project Management Basics* (1990, *Marcel Dekker Inc.*), in the section on inspection of work states: 'Field inspection includes those site activities designed to ensure that the entire facility is faithfully constructed as specified by the engineering documents and results in work that conforms to the owner's expectations.'

Field inspection and testing must first of all be performed by the responsible sub-contractor in accordance with the applicable quality plan and/or specification. These may or may not be witnessed by the managing contractor or client. Field inspection and testing of the entire facility is usually carried out by the managing contractor and the customer.

There are several options that are possible:

- Work as a joint team in order to reduce the costs of additional inspectors that the managing contractor would have had to employ.

- All the field inspections are carried out by the managing contractor with only certain critical inspections being witnessed or carried out by the customer.

- All field inspection is carried out by both managing contractor and the customer as separate exercises. This is not recommended, as it adds substantial costs without adding value.

- Field inspection and testing of statutory items is carried out by a third party inspectorate after initial inspection by the main contractor.

- Field testing of these items should only be done once, with all parties present to witness and accept.

It is necessary to draft and work to a field inspection and test plan which has been accepted by the design, site construction and erection as well as the quality department, of the main contractor. This written plan will need to be reviewed (where necessary modified) and accepted by the customer to ensure comprehensive and acceptable field inspection and terms. It is usually recommended to have this task completed and the plan formally accepted for a particular part of the project before work can commence.

Inspection for preservation of product quality

Once a product's or system's quality has been established and demon-strated, the preservation thereof also requires effort and inspection. There are two main areas that need to be controlled.

- Storage and laydown areas of material and equipment.

- Installed equipment and systems that have to wait for periods in excess of four weeks prior to being commissioned and taken into production.

The areas receiving inspection and the conditions necessary for maintenance of quality while items and material are waiting to be used should be specified by the designer. It is necessary to carry out inspections at regular intervals, usually fortnightly, to ensure that: the conditions are being maintained, and the product quality – in spite of these or other abnormal circumstances – remains within specification.

CASE STUDY:

Fully finished automated butterfly valves were delivered to site on a Saturday morning without warning (the delivery date should have been mutually agreed). The items were in crates which were wrapped in a heavy plastic to prevent the ingress of moisture. The storemen did not have the correct handling equipment to move them into the store, so they were placed in the open air lay-down area on bricks.

That afternoon a severe storm arose, tearing this top outer plastic slightly and allowing some rain in. By Monday everything had dried out on the outside and the valves were moved into the store, and no further inspection was carried out. Three months later when the valves were withdrawn from the store and opened for the 'first time' they were found to be severely rusted and had to be re-worked. The cost of re-work had to be borne by the managing contractor.

It is necessary to draw up a specific schedule for these inspections and assign the responsibility for them to a particular inspector. The condition of these items should be reported on (preferably by exception) on a monthly basis.

The designer or manufacturer of equipment must also specify how its quality is to be maintained while it is waiting to be installed or commissioned. It is also necessary to inspect this equipment at least every two weeks on a busy construction site to ensure there has been no damage or removal of items for other jobs, as well as compliance with other preservation requirements.

The following is a list of some of the items that an inspector will have to inspect for:

- prevention against physical damage i.e. by crates, scaffolding etc.;

- prevention against theft or sabotage (locking items up and/or delaying installing of the valuable, easily removable items, until just before commissioning);

- prevention of ingress of water, dirt or objects i.e. by covering all flanges and closing all openings as well as protecting against the weather and physical damage;

- protection of bearing or rotating surfaces by the use of special anti-rust lubricants and hand rotation on a weekly basis;

- protection of special sealing surfaces by physical protection flanges and anti-corrosion material;

- protection against the elements especially rain, snow, freezing, flooding excess heat or lightning;

- protection against pests such as rodents, termites etc. (especially electrical insulation);

- protection against fire.

Once again it is advisable to draw up a list of the applicable hazards and what the preventive methods will be. An action plan can be drawn up, and an appropriate inspection plan can flow from the action plan.

The pressure of work on the project staff is usually high and consequently these items are often overlooked. A loss at this stage is one of the most expensive losses that can occur because of the delays it will cause at a later stage. It is therefore necessary to assign the responsibility for this inspection activity to a specific team. This activity gradually increases as the plant progresses, and will need more people in order to be able to handle the workload.

On many projects a specific team is employed to inspect the preservation of quality during storage of materials and items awaiting installation. As the project progresses the need for storage inspection reduces while that for installed item inspection increases. This team is already familiar with the preservation needs of the prefabricated items, and is therefore redeployed to continue with installed item preservation as installation progresses.

Inspection decisions and status

The main reason for carrying out an inspection and/or test is to decide whether an item or system conforms to its design specifications. An inspector will have to make certain decisions during and upon completion of the inspection and testing procedures, namely:

- Decide whether the product or system fully conforms to the design specification so that it can be accepted outright;

- Decide whether the product or system is so far from conformation that it should be rejected outright;

- Decide whether a non-conforming product or system is still fit for use and can be used with a concession;

- Decide whether a non-conforming product or system could be repaired and suggest the possibility of re-work;

- Decide where there is evidence of systematic error or even cover up of problems and communicate this to management for corrective action.

The inspector will have to communicate these decisions to management, as well as noting them on the data pack as required by the quality plan. The communication to management is usually in the form of an inspection report, while that to the data pack may only be a signature signing the system off, or it could also include a copy of the inspection report.

Timely and accurate reporting by inspectors to management is very important. The decision to reject or recommend re-work of a system automatically involves the commitment of additional resources to correct the error. The implications of such a decision can have a ripple effect on other areas of the project, and the sooner management knows about it the sooner they can attend to the matter.

It is important to indicate the inspection status of critical and major items and components of a project. This status is important to ensure that work is not carried out on unaccepted or unacceptable items or systems and that these are not inadvertently installed or used. Inspection status is usually indicated by means of tags, signed off copies of the quality plan or even colour codes painted on to or affixed to the item or system. The inspection status indicator or tag usually allows for several conditions which can be clearly indicated through colour coding, signatures, tear-off strips, pass or reject stickers, or stamps on the item or documentation.

The conditions that are usually allowed for are:

- uninspected and awaiting inspection;

- progress inspection, especially where several inspection steps are necessary;

- quarantine where an item is not acceptable and is awaiting a dispositioning decision (where possible these items are placed in a separate quarantine area);

- inspected and accepted;

- inspected and rejected.

It is important to ensure that the inspection status is also communicated to the documentation or configuration data system for inclusion in the configuration status (where applicable).

Calibration

An individual carrying out inspection and testing activities has to make decisions based on observations and measurements. If the measurements are inaccurate because the equipment was inaccurate, even though it was used correctly, then an inspector can make an incorrect decision based on the inaccurate results.

Inspection and test equipment, like any other equipment, is subject to wear and/or deterioration in accuracy during use and in some instances during storage. It is therefore necessary to calibrate all measuring devices against suitable standards with a higher order of accuracy. The rule of thumb is that the measuring instrument should ideally be capable of an accuracy or resolution of ten times better that the tolerance being measured. This is as far as possible applied to calibration equipment, calibrating, measuring and test instruments.

The process of calibration allows for the review, rectification or adjustment of measuring instruments in order to maintain their accuracy. In instances where an instrument cannot be corrected by rectification or adjustment then it must be either downgraded to less accurate work or taken out of commission. The process of calibration takes place under controlled conditions using approved procedures. The responsibility for the calibration of all measuring instruments on a project is usually delegated to the quality department. It is their responsibility to set up calibration procedures and frequencies for all measuring instruments so that the accuracy and repeatability can be assured during the project.

The quality department must establish a full inventory of all the relevant measuring and test instruments that are in use on the project, and formulate a re-call and recalibration procedure and schedule for each one of them.

Many large project contractors have their own calibration laboratories which are accredited by the national calibration system. It is advisable to consider contracting the services of accredited calibration laboratories to perform these functions for the project especially on smaller projects' measuring equipment.

Document handling and control

Documentation as a management communication tool

The communication of information, decisions, contracts, buying orders, designs, work progress reports and many other systems and items used generates significant amounts of documentation from within as well as outside of the project. This information is vital to the management control and progress of the project.

The quality and importance of documentation makes it vital to establish a comprehensive system to handle and control documentation from the earliest activities on a project, vital. During the early phases of a small project a manual system will suffice but in most larger projects computer run systems have definite economic advantages.

It is recommended that a documentation policy be formulated even during the early negotiation phases. Often the documentation just starts to accumulate on the project and before long documents are lost in the piles. It is only after the situation is out of control that some organizations take corrective action when it is too late and can be very costly.

Documentation policy and strategy

A documentation policy and strategy will have to address several basic principles that are required in order to be able to manage the flood of documents and information that will follow later in the project:

- Will documentation handling and control be centralized, decentralized or a combination with centralized master copies and issuing system, using decentralized working copies? The combination of centralized master copies and decentralized working copies is what usually happens in practice, and should be catered for from the beginning.

- What type of documentation identification system will be used? Will it be controlled centrally or will there only be a central register, with activity decentralized identification and registers with notification to central records of new documents?

- What type of back-up system will be used to augment the original hard copy or electronic form? What will the back-up frequency be?

- What type of storage and retrieval system will be used?

- Who will issue approved documents? This is usually the responsibility of the project document control group.

- Who determines the document review and approval flow sheet?

- Who is the first recipient and recorder of all incoming mail? Usually this is handled by central document control and information.

- Who sends out all documentation that leaves the project office? This is often handled by central document control as well.

- What documents must be retained at the end of the project? Documents that need to be retained must meet either one of the following two needs:
  - handover to the customer;
  - retention by the managing contractor for future record and study.

- What is the policy that prevents the unnecessary storage or destruction of documents?

Many large projecting organizations have dealt with these aspects many times and have standard procedures and strategies for addressing these issues. It is often advisable to subcontract this function to a specialist organization to manage professionally and cost effectively.

Identification and codification of documentation

Documentation identification and codification systems also exist based on project activity or discipline. These will be listed in a standard manual and any person (with suitable basic training and planning) generating a document will be able to codify it themselves and register the document and its identification code with the control documentation group.

This code then automatically becomes the storage address for filing and retrieval. If a document codification system is not available or cannot be purchased this should become one of the priority items in the establishment of a documentation system, at the very beginning of a project.

Establishment of facilities and handling procedures for documents

The next step will be to establish procedures for document receipt, duplication and storage. Facilities depending upon the document control systems design have to be acquired and commissioned. Only after these facilities exist can documents be generated, received, moved, stored, issued and used in an orderly manner. The optimization of the documentation flow and handling can now be carried out effectively.

Salkovitch in Section 5 of *Project Management Basics* (1989, Marcel Dekker Inc.) points out that documentation flow sheets which show the path of distribution and all associated recording and control functions can be developed. He points out that these activities usually include the following:

- document receipt;
- date stamping and logging;
- distribution of copies for review;
- expediting review comments;
- co-ordinating comments;
- finalizing comments;
- customer's approvals (as required);
- issue of approved documents;
- location of project file copies.

It is important to record the document's codification (identity) as well as its status.

Incoming mail is usually handled by the central documentation group and is date stamped in order to log its arrival. It is then forwarded in accordance with the documentation flow system and procedures. There are many documents that are supplied by material or equipment suppliers which have a bearing on quality. They can take the form of material analysis or performance test reports and are often additional source documents. These are also important and must be included in the system.

Documentation log book

Log books are usually developed (manual or electronic) for each of the main categories of documentation so that day to day transactions as well as a record of documentation generated can be kept. Log books also record the document identification, code name revision and approval status. This helps ensure that there are no duplicate identifications registered. The log book also records the total documentation generated and registered within a specific project discipline or activity.

Monthly analysis and progress reporting

It is advisable to perform an analysis of the status of each of the various categories of documents that are being controlled. This analysis should be performed and reported on a monthly basis, and be given high visibility by either posting to all the relevant managers or even posting it up outside the document control office (or both). This report can be expanded to form a progress chart for each document that is generated in the various project activities.

The progress chart could indicate the following and allow everybody to be aware of the progress of the document, be it a procedure, purchase requisition, specification, etc.

- issue status;

- approval requirements and status;

- review status and who must review;

- amounts of comments;

- progress with corrections;

- dates of approval;

- to whom originals were issued.

This progress report will enable all interested parties to ascertain almost at a glance what the progress with, and status of, all significant documents on the project is. Effective document generation, management and control is a key element in the successful management of projects.

Benchmarking

Benchmarking is defined by Rank Xerox, the organization that first actively developed and employed the technique, as 'the continuous process of measuring products, services and processes against strongest competitors or those renowned as world leaders in their field'.

Benchmarking also employs an external focus to search out the best of the best and adopt, as well as adapt these processes and procedures to the organization in order to utilize the best known methods of performing a task. This forms part of the basis of continuous improvement. The intention is not only to equal, but also to better these methods in order to achieve world class quality and productivity.

Benchmarking can be used in the project environment for two reasons.

- The achieving and exceeding of the best known methods of performing work (including management).

- The seeking out of the best plants and facilities or parts thereof and where possible incorporating them into design and deployment of the project facilities or systems, in order to maximize project effectiveness and customer satisfaction.

Many books have been written on this subject and there are 'benchmarking clearing houses' in many countries which can be used by project managers in order to ascertain what the benchmark process or procedure for a particular activity is.

CHAPTER EIGHT

The phases of and participants in projects

The activities of a project that become visible to an uninvolved outsider are really the visible tip of the figurative iceberg, with all the initial ideas, activities, preparations and calculations, etc., being the bulk of the effort and brain power that has to be put into a project, before the visible parts can take shape.

The phases and activities

Projects usually start with a need or an opportunity that is established or that presents itself, sometimes by chance, or by tragedy, or even one that has been created by creative or pro-active marketing. Sometimes the closing of the doors of a previous opportunity or solution to a need necessitates the creation of an alternative solution in the form of products or services.

The solution of these problems or the satisfying of their needs, starts with ideas and concepts that have been conceived by an individual or a 'think tank' or team. The ideas and conceptual solutions at this stage are kept alive and nurtured by a champion of the idea or by an active working group which believes that a particular solution has the basic elements needed for success.

The validity of the market needs, as well as the conceptual solutions to these problems and needs, often do not find ready acceptance on a broad commercial and technical front. It is very often the champion (be it an individual or a team) of these solutions that has to carry the torch or nurture the concept through these stages. He/she has to obtain enough credible information about the magnitude, requirements, limitations and opportunities of the need, to interest and convince the decision makers that the opportunities of the concept warrant the investment of enough venture capital to perform a pre-feasibility study of needs or opportunities and possible conceptual solutions.

Many potentially viable projects never see the 'lights of the boardroom' because the requirements for a project's market and customer needs survey are not fully appreciated and addressed.

These requirements are not only in terms of a clear credible establishment of what the market needs in terms of requirements and deliverables are, but also the information that potential investors would require before they are prepared to commit any (or future) venture capital. In many instances, the effort required to conduct or obtain the information from a market survey, as well as the formulation and examination of the conceptual solutions, is done by the champion/s of the concept in their own time (albeit overtime – if they are employed by a company that will possibly fund the later stages) because their belief in the opportunity (or need) and the conceptual solutions is their own self-motivator. This phase is, therefore, a no budget or 'handle within existing budget' activity. Often a large proportion of the man hours and sometimes even some of the expenses are carried by the champion/s personally.

It is for these reasons that when quality in projects or, in other words, the factors that influence the carrying out of a project correctly (which in the opinion of the author is basically the same concept) are considered, all the factors influencing the quality of the project should be established right from the earliest stages.

It is also axiomatic that a potentially good project which never reached the stage of basic assessment regarding its possibilities, because the requirements and deliverables of the potentially interested parties who could fund such an assessment had never been met or established, can also be regarded as a 'miscarriage of quality'.

Once the economic and technical potential of a market need and solution has been realized and the decision to perform a basic assessment (both technically and economically) has been taken, then it is also essential to establish what the requirements and deliverables for the basic assessment attributes are. This is necessary so that the results of this assessment have the maximum opportunity of having a potentially successful project accepted for a feasibility study.

It is also important to note that failure to satisfy these requirements and deliverables when questionable projects are reviewed should also automatically lead to rejection of the project, or, at very best, the decision to obtain clarity on certain issues before the feasibility study can commence.

In instances where large or high risk/reward projects are under consideration, it is often necessary to carry out a pre-feasibility study in order to clarify areas of uncertainty and risk, before an expensive feasibility study can be undertaken. Failure to accept a potentially good project or to reject a questionable one for a feasibility study, are both failures in the correct preparation of these presentations, and therefore also represent miscarriages of quality.

It is for these reasons that management for quality (or in other words management to do the right thing at the right time) must be involved in projects from the earliest stages. It must also be appreciated that the term management for quality constitutes the actions to be taken by the various parties responsible for taking the lead during the various activities of the pre-project (or any other) phase. Many of the omissions and incorrect (or only partially correct) assumptions made, or principles used during the pre-project phase, carry through into the project execution and even operational phase, with very serious cost, time and operational consequences.

It is very important that each activity of each phase, and especially the pre-project phase, be critically and formally reviewed for possible errors to ensure that they are picked up and eliminated at their source, thereby minimizing the resultant cost of this error, should it be carried forward into the project. The importance and thoroughness of establishing the requirements and deliverables for each activity cannot be over emphasized as the 'real world' will definitely show up errors if they exist.

The management for quality in projects must therefore be involved in the pre-project phase in the following activities (with the specified persons or groups holding the reins of leadership and control during the various phases):

PRE-PROJECT PHASE		
	Activities where quality should be involved	Leadership and control
1.	Basic assessment	Concept champion and mentor
2.	Pre-feasibility study	Study team including champion, potential investor and operator
3.	Feasibility study	Full professional feasibility study team, including potential managing contractors and plant operators, etc.

The project execution phase has very well-known activities which relate to the natural sequence of events and it is felt that it is not necessary to have to justify the involvement of quality as it is self-evident.

PROJECT EXECUTION PHASE		
	Activities where quality is involved	Leadership and control
4.	Engineering design and technical issues	Managing contractors, plant operators and owners
5.	Procurement of supplies	Managing contractor
6.	Construction and erection	Managing contractor supported by suppliers and sub-contractors at their respective level of involvement, i.e. quality is a line responsibility with assessment of achievement of systems and milestones as a staff support by a quality management group
7.	Precommission handover	Managing contractor assisted by operations team (production, maintenance)
8.	Commissioning	
9.	Contract and project close-out	

A project can only be classified a success when the facility it created is functionally successful, which was the ultimate reason for utilizing the quality principles from the earliest activities of the project.

It is, therefore, necessary, that the operations phase also be considered, as many operational needs can only be addressed during the feasibility study or the engineering design and technical activities and thereafter they must be built into the plant as a natural product of the design.

OPERATIONS PHASE		
	Activities where quality is involved	Leadership and control
10.	Start up	Operations, commissioning and maintenance team(s)
11.	De-bottlenecking and trouble-shooting	Operations, commissioning and maintenance team(s)
12.	Operational optimization	Operations and maintenance
13.	Decommissioning	Operations and decommissioning contractor

The estimated cost ratios of non-quality

The correction of errors on a project is costly, and the price of poor quality can often break a project and make it uneconomical. Estimates of the cost and cost escalation (with progress on the project) of correcting errors are as follows:

Phase and activity of the project	Cost to correct
Pre-Project Phase	
Basic assessment	Unity $\times$ 2
– market and customer need	Unity
– initial concept	Unity
Pre-feasibility study	Unity $\times$ 4
Feasibility study	Unity $\times$ 8
Project Execution Phase	
Engineering design (technical)	Unity $\times$ 16
Procurement of supplies	Unity $\times$ 32
Construction and erection	Unity $\times$ 50 to 100
Precommissioning and handover	Unity $\times$ 100
Commissioning	Unity $\times$ 100
Project close-out	Unity $\times$ 100
Operations Phase	
Plant or system start up	Unity $\times$ 100
De-bottlenecking and troubleshooting	Unity $\times$ 150
Operation and Optimization (including lost production)	Unity $\times$ 200 to 500
Decommissioning	Unity $\times$ 200

A study of the table on estimated cost of correcting errors will emphasize the necessity of avoiding and/or eliminating errors as early as possible because the further the error progresses undetected into the project, the more expensive it – and its consequences – become to correct.

It is for all of these reasons that the full list of phases and their activities should be considered when a list of requirements and deliverables (which form the basis for managing for quality) is being formulated.

The parties involved in projects

Projects are all about people and life, and creating functional and viable solutions to human needs as well as those of other life or even beauty forms. It is the people, rather than companies or organizations, who make things happen successfully. Organizations and companies (and their people) are conduits that empower and facilitate individuals in their goal of making the project come about successfully. The opposite can also be true, namely, that an organization and the individuals of the organization can disempower and frustrate others in their attempts at a successful project.

It is, therefore, important to identify who plays a meaningful role in a project and at what stage they are involved. The timeous and correct involvement of these people is essential if all the pertinent requirements and deliverables necessary for success are to be established and quantified in a pro-active manner.

Earlier in this chapter the functionaries who play a major role in making the various activities 'happen successfully' were listed with the activity. A short list of 'key promoters' (actively involved parties) can be identified from this list of functionaries, namely:

- concept champion, mentor or initiator;

- suppliers of capital (venture or project capex);

- project initiators and/or study team;

- managing contractors (and sub-contractors);

- plant owners;

- plant operators.

There are also other involved parties who are drawn into a project re-actively, but who nevertheless play an important role. Although these parties are involved re-actively, their contribution (or requirements) can have a profound impact on the formulation of some of the requirements and deliverables (i.e. on quality).

The list of influential involved parties includes:

- licensors of processes and equipment;

- government and local authorities (and associated regulations);

- environmentalists (and the environment).

There are some people who are involved in a more indirect and passive manner and whose requirements and deliverables also have an influence on the project. These passive parties include:

- shareholders (where share-rights are issued);

- individuals who are employed or otherwise affected by the facility (that the project sets out to create) after the project has been completed (stakeholders).

These three lists are indicative only and while they represent those who are usually involved, different projects may require the involvement of more (or less) than those on these lists.

From these lists it can be seen that some of the involved parties overlap in their involvement and others are more independent. It is, therefore, necessary to establish which parties are usually involved and at what stage, so that they can be consulted/utilized timeously in order to help ensure a better quality of project (i.e. better establishment of, and conformance to, requirements and deliverables).

A summary of activities and deliverables for the various project phases

The inter-relationship of phases and activities with the involved parties can best be expressed as a matrix which sets down in broad generic terms (and which has to be made project specific) what all the requirements and deliverables are for each activity (of each phase) and for each of the involved parties.

Very often the problems with quality in projects arise not with the requirements and deliverables that have been fully identified and quantified, but rather with those that have been overlooked or partly or even incorrectly identified and quantified. The following tables give the reader a generic list and the nature of the involvement. Flowing from this, the more specific activities and deliverables, which quantify what must happen and what the desired end-result should be, can be identified.

Therefore, Table 8.4(a) must be read as a total concept. The same is applicable for Tables 8.4(b), etc.

TABLE 8.4: The summary of activities and deliverables for the pre-project phase.

These three activities can be expanded upon in the following manner:

TABLE 8.4(a)(i)

	Activities	Deliverables of each Activity Stage
1.0	**Basic assessment: The creative pre-budget, loosely, structured activity**	
1.1	Market or customer evaluation	Quantified and specified market needs/opportunities
1.2	Initial concept	Original concepts of possible solutions
1.3	Evaluation of concepts and recommendations for pre-feasibility study	Short ranking of concepts based on cost estimates and economic evaluations
		Recommendation for a pre-feasibility study (or abort activity) including plans and budget for pre-feasibility study
2.0	**Pre-feasibility study: The evaluative, controlled, disciplined and budgeted activity**	
2.1	Evaluate all options from basic assessment	Narrow options down to two or three only
2.2	Study of each option in terms of	
	– raw materials	List raw materials required as available
	– product slate	Product slate of each option considered
	– size of facility	Quantify size based on operational options
	– location	Position of facility relative to materials and market
	– type of technology	Selected specific technology
	– environment	Environmental impact study of options
	– demography, etc.	Demographic study of project

TABLE 8.4(a)(i)   *Continued*

	Activities	*Deliverables of each Activity Stage*
2.3	Evaluation of economic viability Competitiveness in the market place	A report detailing the economic viability and competitiveness
2.4	Obtain appropriate inputs from – potential financiers – potential owners – potential operators	Willingness to finance such a project, both Capex and Opex, needed Possibility of setting up an owner together with the operational feasibility of options
2.5	Documented conclusion for consideration by Board of Directors, etc. Propose the best option (one only). Establish all the requirements, deliverables, project scope, budget, schedule and quality requirements for the feasibility study	Propose the best option for consideration. List all requirements of the option. List the deliverables of the best option. Document, detailing the project scope. Proposal to include budget and schedule needed for the feasibility study. List of general requirements and specifications for deliverables and possible milestones

3.0   Feasibility Study: The determinative activity focused, disciplined, budgeted and reviewed

3.1	Confirm the scope given by the pre-feasibility study	Specifically approved detailed scope
3.2	A full technical financial schedule and quality study of the single option decided upon	Feasibility study report covering, detailing and quantifying all aspects
3.3	A full project execution planning and scheduling, as well as their influence on quality study of the single option decided upon	A full project execution plan

TABLE 8.4(a)(ii)

Activities	*Deliverables of each Activity Stage*
1.0 Basic Assessment	
1.1 Market and customer needs To establish all the market related requirements and deliverables that must be researched and reported upon by the involved parties.	A complete 'stand alone' report detailing market studies as well as the potential initial pay-back period and market viability. Detail market's quality needs in terms of deliverables and specifications. The potential environmental impact of the product, plant and project must also be reported.
1.2 Initial concept To initiate a process that will propose creative solutions for the market needs and arrive at a most feasible first and second option to consider.	A report detailing the various concepts that have been suggested with their advantages as well as their disadvantages. From these concepts the two best options and the reasons for their choice must be developed.
1.3 Evaluation of concepts and recommendation To review the initial concept proposed in terms of possible plant options, constructability, pay-back periods, acceptability of the technology required as well as profitability. Recommend or reject a pre-feasibility or direct feasibility study.	If the pre-feasibility study is recommended the report must include the budget, resources, planning and schedule for such a study, so that an informed decision can be taken. If the pre-feasibility is rejected then the reasons for rejection must be detailed in the report.

TABLE 8.4(a)(ii)   *Continued*

Activities	*Deliverables of each Activity Stage*
2.0 Pre-feasibility study	
Review the concept proposed in the basic assessment and establish the areas of uncertainty. Determine whether they can be met with existing technology and where special work and requirements will have to be confirmed. (This is usually only performed on large or borderline projects).	Pre-feasibility study report detailing all the unknown factors or problem areas. It must also propose solutions to these so that the achievability of the project can be assessed on a broad base. This will also include a review of the availability of licensed process, etc. that can be used in the project. Problematic or special areas with special requirements or quality needs must also be highlighted.
3.0 Feasibility study	
To finalize the project scope, the general engineering and design that will be needed to address all requirements and problems of the project. This will include a full cost and planning analysis so that project costs as well as return on investment and pay-back periods can be established. (This does not include detail design, etc. of the project.) Special attention must be paid to specifying requirements, standards and deliverables as well as the cost and planning implications.	A separate 'stand alone' report that addresses all the objectives of this activity stage. This report must also comment on the feasibility of the project concept examined and give clear reasons why the project is considered to be feasible or not. This report must also include a special section examining the risk and how these can be designed out, or minimized.

TABLE 8.4(b)(i) The Summary of Activities and Deliverables for the Project Execution Phase

The following six activities of this phase can be expanded in the following manner:

Activities	Deliverables of each Activity Stage
4.0 Engineering and technical design: This is where the parameters and project scope of the feasibility studies are converted into detail requirements and specifications. This is where quality is designed and engineered in pro-activity.	
4.1 Perform detail engineering design	Discrete, complete, reviewed and approved design packages
4.2 Establish the specifications and procedures	Approved procedures and specification sheets
4.3 Issue purchasing and construction packages	Discrete, reviewed and approved packages containing data sheets, specifications, bills of quantity and drawings, etc.
5.0 Procurement of supplies: This is the start of converting ideas into services and hardware. The rapid commitment of resources begins, and control is needed to ensure value for money.	
5.1 Establish a procurement system that will consistently procure acceptable (quality) goods and services, i.e. that will give value for money	A system that uses approved vendors to obtain tenders for the whole system sought and that ensures good communication of all requirements for achievement of financial technical quality and project acceptability of procured items.
5.2 Progressively assess that the quality of purchased items is acceptable	Approved quality systems and plans, interim inspection reports and finally accepted data packages, which arrive with the procured items (including change control)
5.3 Acceptance and payment only for correct or quality items	Goods receipt, report and authorization for payment of fully acceptable and documented goods.

TABLE 8.4(b)(i) *Continued*

Activities	*Deliverables of each Activity Stage*
6.0 Construction and erection: This phase converts materials, components, systems and services into an integrated functional plant	
6.1 Establish an integrated management system for quality	A system that ensures that the people responsible for performing a task know and are equipped for the following: – a contract or brief that indicates that they understand the deliverables and requirements – quality plans addressing the interim activities and their quality requirements that will result in an acceptable plant and sub-system – progressively assess compliance with the quality plans – only pay for fully acceptable (quality) and docmented deliverables
6.2 Assess that all the requirements and specifications have been met	Progressively signed off and accepted quality plans. Quality audit reports confirming the successful use of the system. Inspection and test reports confirming that all technical requirements have been met.
6.3 Confirm and document for future reference that all the quality requirements have been met	Final close-out acceptance of the full data packages of each system or sub-system contracted. These must be commensurate with the system's use and impact on the operational facility.
7.0 Precommissioning and handover: This phase prepares the constructed system for handover to the customer and commissioning team. (It also documents the acceptability).	
7.1 Clean the plant physically and also, where necessary from a process point of view	A clean plant or facility both internally and externally that is free from dangerous debris

TABLE 8.4(b)(i)   *Continued*

	Activities	Deliverables of each Activity Stage
7.2	Operate or turn over all equipment with moving parts	A plant that is able to correctly use or operate its moving equipment, i.e. valves, pumps, motors, actuators, etc.
7.3	Check that all controls are functional	A plant that can be monitored and controlled by the instrumentation and control equipment
7.4	Energize the plant	All systems energized safely and controllably
8.0	**Commissioning: This activity brings the plant into operation in a very controlled manner so as not to cause damage.**	
8.1	Plan the commissioning sequence and controls	Commissioning plan
8.2	Draft the commissioning procedures	A complete list of formally reviewed and accepted procedures
8.3	Commission the plant in accordance with the plan and procedures	A commissioned functional plant with acceptance documentation
9.0	**Contract and project close-out: This is the final rounding off and completion of all the outstanding formalities of the contract including reports, final corrections and final payment against fully acceptable (quality milestones and deliverables) plant or system**	
9.1	Comparison of what was received with what was ordered in terms of requirements and specifications	A final acceptance report confirming that all requirements have been complied with and documented
9.2	Settlement of the final claims against acceptable deliverables and/or mutually negotiated concessions and variations	A formal review mechanism and board representing all parties affected by the deliverables, that confirms acceptability for payment or part-payment/ retention

TABLE 8.4(c)(i) The summary of activities and deliverables for the operational phase

Activities	Deliverables of each Activity Stage
10.0 Start up: This formally extends the commissioning into the semi-continuous and ultimately continuous operation of the facility	
10.1 Run the plant with both contractor and operational crew with a view to final handover of operations	An operational plant or system that delivers sufficient product that is on specification
10.2 Formally hand the plant over to operations	A handover document and operational and maintenance procedure accepted by both project management and operations, that demonstrates that the system functions in accordance with all the requirements and can continue to function and be maintained
11.0 De-bottlenecking and Troubleshooting: This activity increases the productivity, availability and reliability of the facility	
11.1 A full study of the plant performance and the problem areas experienced during operation	A report on the study highlighting the problem areas, comparing the plant to benchmark equivalents and proposing corrective action
11.2 Progressively implement the proposed improvements	A fully productive efficient plant with high availability producing consistently acceptable product (or service)

TABLE 8.4(c)(i) *Continued*

Activities	Deliverables of each Activity Stage

12.0 Operation and optimization: Where the performance of the plant, its feedstock maintenance and products are gradually optimized

12.1 A continuous plant performance analysis taking, among other factors, the following into account: – process robustness (ability to withstand variation) – plant safety – product quality – quality cost and availability of feed – maintenance costs – plant availability – feed and waste costs – environment	A profitable, environmentally safe, acceptable plant or system, that consistently produces acceptable products

13.0 Decommissioning: Taking an operating plant out of operation in a safe and reliable manner and resulting in a safe, environmentally friendly, stationary facility or system

13.1 Take the plant out of operation to achieve one or a combination of the following: A plant that is 'mothballed' safely and that can be re-started with a minimum of risk and cost A plant that can receive major repair, modification or refurbishment A plant that can cost effectively be demolished safely	A decommissioning manual supported by procedures and work instructions to safely decommission a plant facility to achieve one of the listed end results

TABLE 10.4(c)(ii)

Activities	Deliverables of each Activity Stage

10.0 Start up

The operational integration of all the systems and sub-systems of a plant or product for continuous or semi-continuous operation	A fully functional plant or system delivering a product or service that meets specifications and requirements (ie. a quality product or service)

11.0 De-bottlenecking and troubleshooting

To study the (as built) plant design, capacities and layout from an operational point of view, using a benchmark plant as a reference point, where possible. This exercise must also be carried out on the operational plant to ensure optimum operating conditions	A full report on the study highlighting potential problem areas taking the following into account: – Areas of under capacity – Areas of low availability – Areas where product, service specifications or quality are not achievable or maintainable – High risk areas (safety or otherwise) – The report should include action plans for improvement

12.0 Operation and optimization

A detailed study of the operating plant in order to optimize through-put rates in terms of product quality and consistency as well as system safety, reliability and maintainability	A full report on the optimum operating conditions. This report is supported by the operational results, procedures and training schedules needed to establish and ensure maintenance of these conditions

13.0 Decommissioning

To establish the best decommissioning and 'mothballing' extensive refurbishment or demolition procedures	A report and system detailing how the plant should be decommissioned optimally for: 1. 'Mothballing' 2. Extensive changes 3. Demolition

PART 4

Matrix

CHAPTER NINE

The matrix relating project phases and involved parties/ disciplines

Introduction

The purpose of this chapter is to develop a matrix of interrelationships between the requirements, deliverables and activities of the various phases and the various parties that are involved (or potentially involved) in a project.

In Chapter 8 the various phases of a project are discussed and the generally applicable activities of each phase, together with the parties who would typically initiate or lead/manage each activity, are listed. When the phases and their activities are listed vertically (numerically) and the potentially involved parties are listed horizontally (alphabetically) then an alpha-numeric matrix can be formed. Each block on the matrix indicates whether there is an interrelationship or not.

It is important to note that the matrix is not intended to be the 'alpha and omega' of all possible combinations of involvement. It needs to be made project-specific and expanded (or contracted) according to the project needs.

Layout of the project management matrix

This matrix is designed as an *'aide-mémoire'* or memory jogger when establishing the requirements and deliverables that form the basis for quality on projects.

The first two blocks of each row across give the objectives and the deliverables of each activity of a particular phase. The involved parties who are referred to in each row across are the people who are most likely to play a role and consequently who will have:

- requirements and deliverables of their own that the project should meet;

- a role to play in the project in terms of developing, formulating and communicating and often achieving these requirements and deliverables.

A summary of all the requirements and deliverables of all the involved parties in a particular activity of a phase will give the total of the requirements and deliverables to be met for that activity and should, as a minimum, add up to the deliverables for each row across.

The various activities of each phase give an indication of the status of the project and by implication, the status of involvement of the various parties and of their input and expectations as well as progress, as the project proceeds through the various activities of each phase. There should be a natural progression of requirements and deliverables for each involved party, as each activity of each phase progresses (i.e. progression down the matrix numerically).

The summary of all the activities of each phase, for each involved party, must also add up to the total picture that needs to be addressed and satisfied by each involved party at the final activity of each phase. Therefore, for the pre-project phase, these must add up to the total list of requirements and deliverables of the feasibility study. The sum of the activities of the involved parties in the project execution phase must add up to the contract and project close-out activities.

It is important to note that the description given in each block of the matrix is a generic summary in order to help the reader as an 'aide-mémoire'. These terms should be made project-specific, with the aid of a suitably qualified team, in a workshop or in brain-storm session/s. The matrix could then be likened to a printer's tray for each activity, with a drawer per activity housing the typical deliverables of that activity.

In specific projects it will often be necessary to add to or (more likely) to delete from the number of activities of a phase, depending upon the size, complexity and unknown factors of that phase. It is also possible that there are projects which will not only involve extra but also different parties from those listed and once again a 'workshop' activity is recommended to ensure that all the relevant parties are involved from the earliest stages of a project.

The blank spaces on the matrix indicate no expected involvement during that activity with a particular party. This can, however, change from project to project, and the project co-ordinator or manager is advised to make sure that this is still applicable for the particular project in question. The information printed in the blocks of the matrix gives the generic requirements, deliverables and activity of the respective involved party for a particular activity of a particular phase.

Use of the matrix detail

It must be stressed that this information is the 'generic what'. The involved parties must convert it into the 'project-specific what' and thereafter their own form of 'how' in order to satisfy the requirements, and thus produce an acceptable deliverable, with the appropriate forms of measurement in order to confirm achievement of the deliverable. Care must be taken by the activity co-ordinator to ensure that the sum of all the requirements and deliverables of a particular activity, as a minimum, conforms to the project-specific requirements and deliverables for that activity.

The involved party/ies must also ensure that the progression of their requirements through any project will also add up to the total or ultimate requirement and deliverable for that particular involved party at the end of the specific phase.

This matrix is not intended to be the starting point for the generation of multiple procedures and work instructions, but to give a practical indication of what project managers need to keep in mind and do when the various phases of the project are being undertaken, in order that key issues are not inadvertently overlooked which can add to or cause other problems.

In certain instances project management may decide that certain procedures will need full development because of the direct applicability and importance of a certain section of the matrix. There could well be many other parts of the matrix that result in only the inclusion of an item on a checklist and require no further documentation.

It is necessary to be careful not to try and generate procedures for every section of the matrix. Care must be taken to ensure that only the necessary documentation for quality on the project is generated as a result of the items on the matrix. Failure to exercise discipline in this regard could result in the conversion of what is intended to be a management aid, to a bureaucratic nightmare, which will result in a total loss of credibility of the quality management system that is developed.

Quality related requirements and deliverables for a project matrix of activity sequence and involved parties

	INVOLVED PARTIES (who) ACTIVITY SEQUENCE (when)		A CUSTOMER
	PRE-PROJECT PHASE Objectives	Deliverables	
1.0 1.1	Basic assessment Market and customer needs: To establish all the market related requirements and deliverables that must be researched and reported upon by the involved parties.	A complete 'stand alone' report detailing market studies as well as the potential market viability. Detail of market's quality needs in terms of deliverables and specifications. The potential environmental impact of the product, plant and project must also be reported.	1.1A Identify market needs and verify by means of market analysis. This includes product slate and future consumption trends. Identify market's environmental reaction to projects and waste and verify by means of independent market analysis. This includes product slate and future consumption trends. Identify market's environmental reaction to products and waste.
1.2	Initial Concept: To initiate a process that will propose creative solutions for the market needs and arrive at a most feasible first and second option to consider.	A report detailing the various concepts that have been suggested with their advantages as well as their disadvantages. From these concepts the two best options and the reasons for their choice must be developed.	1.2A Evaluate possible concepts formally, in a positive factor, negative factor and nett balance concept. Assess customer and general public acceptability of concept on social and environmental impact of product and waste.
1.3	Evaluation of concepts and recommendations: To review the initial concept proposed in terms of possible plant options, constructability pay-back periods, acceptability of the technology required as well as profitability. Recommend the best two other options to be studied together. A proposal budget and schedule for a pre-feasibility study (or propose abandonment).	A report which discusses the details of the favoured concept/s from the point of view of the various items discussed in the objective. This report will confirm or otherwise the real viability of a concept/s.	1.3A Check accuracy of needs by independent formal review. Convert requirements into formal deliverables and their specifications in order to satisfy customer's independent review of feasibility of requirement specifications.
2.0	Pre-feasibility study: Review the concept/s proposed in the basic assessment and establish the areas of uncertainty and determine whether they can be met with existing technology, and where special work and requirements will have to be confirmed. (This is usually only performed on large or borderline projects.) Choose a single best option for the feasibility study.	Pre-feasibility study report detailing all the unknown factors of problem areas. It must also propose solutions to these so that the achievability of the project can be assessed on a broad base. This will also include a review of the availability of licensed process, etc. that can be used in the project. Problematic or special areas with special requirements or quality needs must also be highlighted. Propose the single best option for the feasibility study including the economics of the options.	2.0A Review and confirm whether customer's requirements can be met by all concept/s under consideration. Can customer requirements be modified to make concept feasible? Does sum of deliverables add up to customer satisfaction? Use survey to determine.
3.0	Feasibility study: To finalize the project scope the general engineering and design that will be needed to address all requirements and problems of the project. This will include a full cost and planning analysis so that project costs as well as ROI and pay-back periods can be established. (This does not include detail design, etc. of the project.) Special attention must be paid to specifying requirements, standards and deliverables as well as the cost and planning implications.	A separate 'stand alone' report that addresses all the objectives of this activity stage. This report must also comprehensively study all aspects of the impact on the feasibility of the project concept/s examined and give clear commercial and technical reasons why the project is considered feasible or not.	3.0A Define project scope and confirm that all deliverables satisfy the customer's needs. Review project scope by independent party.

B INVESTORS and SHAREHOLDERS	C PLANT OWNERS	D LICENSORS
1.1B Establish market opportunities and potential. Review findings for accuracy. Determine interested parties and advantages to them.	1.1C Establish product requirements and convert these to intermediate and final product specifications and tests that will ensure customer satisfaction.	1.1D Evaluate ability of licensors who can meet the customer's needs in terms of quality and quantity. Demonstrate ability of process to perform under prevailing circumstances and constraints.
1.2B Perform in-house study to establish criteria for requirements. Specify format that criteria and study report should take. Approve contents list of final report.	1.2C Obtain input and review on: Operability, safety, reliability and constant quality of feed product and waste of the various concepts under consideration.	1.2D Are the initial concepts compatible with the licensed process and design?
1.3B Establish key quality issues in the process of being assessed such as feed materials, process products and waste. Determine and highlight their impact on product slate, construction and operational costs, including cost of waste and also that the risk of those requirements is acceptable from an investment point of view.	1.3C Conduct formal assessment of proposed concept's ability to deliver quality product and waste. (This should also be done by an independent group.)	1.3D Assess possibility of modifying licensed process to meet the concept/s under consideration, or to optimize the concept for prevailing local conditions.
2.0B Include special cost and profit as well as implications of specific quality requirements and deliverables. Confirm achievability, reliability of process and equipment considered and cost implications thereof.	2.0C Establish and review the functional baseline and performance requirements of the preferred concept.	2.0D Ensure by experiment and other methods that any modification to a licensed process will give quality products and waste. The licensor to supply full reports on tests carried out
3.0B Stress involvement of quality from the very beginning. Organizational and personnel requirements and cost must be defined and cost implications high-lighted. Make quality an integral part of report to shareholders.	3.0C Require and ensure that all new concepts and methods be identified and qualified by means of pilot plant tests.	3.0D Conduct independent review that all licensed processes will satisfy customer and plant specifications. Ensure that acceptance tests are properly controlled and relevant.

		E PLANT OPERATORS	F GOVERNMENT and LOCAL AUTHORITIES	G PROJECT MANAGERS
1.0 1.1		1.1E Assess ability to consistently produce quality products and waste.	1.1F Determine whether there are statutes or controls which may affect the use of marketing or disposal of the product or service needed (both present and future).	1.1G Establish an information handling index and system to capture and store relevant information in a retrievable fashion by caretaker project management team.
1.2		1.2E Obtain input on: formal review on operability, safety, reliability and constant quality of feed, product and waste of the various concepts under consideration.	1.2F Take any requirements of F1 into account and incorporate into initial concept proposals.	1.2G
1.3		1.3E Give input as to plant operability (given a specific process) and product slate. Review services needed. Review feed and waste materials and influence on quality of product and waste.	1.3F Establish total impact of laws, by-laws, statutes, etc. on the proposed project. Estimate the relevance and influence of future statutes.	1.3G Basic assessment champion or manager to propose best options as well as a budget, plan and schedule for the pre-feasibility study (or propose abandoning the project).
2.0		2.0E Formulate operability and maintainability requirements. Report on optimization with existing or benchmark plant, where possible.	2.0F Ensure that all plant locations, feed product and waste specifications will conform to these requirements.	2.0G
3.0		3.0E Perform hazard and operations studies and/or failure mode and effect analysis. Review plant maintainability and needs as well as personnel requirements. Perform environmental and social impact studies.	3.0F Involve the affected government and local authorities in the feasibility study and recommendations. Commence with the PR programme.	3.0G Involve potential project management team at this phase in order to bring them up to speed so that they can bid more realistically.

H ENVIRONMENT	I CONSULTANTS
1.1H Review environmental impact of new product and establish environment reaction from the customer. Review impact of waste and its treatment on the environment.	1.1I Use independent consultants to review market and needs assessment. Carry out literature study of possible environmental impact scenarios. Advise on any statutes that can affect the project.
1.2H Take any requirements of H1.1 into account and incorporate into initial concept proposals.	1.2I
1.3H Perform preliminary, environmental study on impact of proposed product, plant and waste.	1.3I Review basic assessment reports for acceptability and errors. Conduct assessment of the plant's ability.
2.0H Establish environmental requirements of the product, plant and waste from a full environmental study.	2.0I Critically review study by independent consultants for error in order to minimize risks.
3.0H Make the environmental requirements part of the total requirements and include in the feasibility study.	3.0I Critically review study (by independent consultants) for error in order to minimize risk areas.

Quality related requirements and deliverables for a project matrix of activity sequence and involved parties

	INVOLVED PARTIES (who) ACTIVITY SEQUENCE (when)		A CUSTOMER
	PROJECT EXECUTION PHASE Objectives	Deliverables	
4.0	Engineering Design and Technical (E D and T): To perform all the detail engineering design as well as establish all the specifications, drawings (and procedures) and other technical information needed to convert the project scope into a procurable and 'constructable' project.	A full design package, including all design assumptions, calculations and independent design reviews, indicating design acceptability. This shall, as a minimum, include all relevant levels of drawings from general lay-outs to detail designs. All specifications and deliverables as well as the necessary quality standards, control and assurance requirements.	4.0A Utilize project scope and deliverables as part of the basic input for the baseline for engineering design.
5.0	Procurement of supplies: To determine and establish a procurement system that will procure goods and services that conform to the design requirements every time, on time and within budget.	A procurement management system that is able to cost effectively procure the necessary goods and services that conform to the specified requirements every time. This will, as a minimum, have systems for the following: Purchasing only from approved suppliers. Purchasing in accordance with the design specification. Demonstrating that all goods received are of acceptable quality. Demonstrating that stored items will maintain their integrity.	5.0A Establish if there are preferred suppliers or brands on the market which are more acceptable to the final customer.
6.0	Construction and erection: To design and establish a construction and erection system that will be able to construct and erect all the purchased parts and site fabrications into an operational plant or system.	A construction and erection management system and manual, including procedures and other necessary communication review systems and demonstrations that will ensure that the construction of the plant or facility meets the design everytime.	6.0A
7.0	Precommission and handover: To plan and list all the activities needed to prepare a plant or system for active service (commissioning) once it has been completed and the functional components tested and approved.	Precommissioning manual detailing the appropriate approach to be followed, the procedures and documentation to be used, when a completed plan or system is prepared to be brought into use.	7.0A Establish a saleable commissioning product slate and customers, with an acceptable market specification.
8.0	Commissioning: To plan and list all the activities including tests and checks (safety and operational) needed, to bring a plant or system into operation for the first time (or after major maintenance) successfully.	A commissioning manual detailing all the management and operational aspects needed to successfully bring a plant or system into operation. This will amongst others, include special quality, safety, operating checks, procedures and documentation to be used during commissioning.	8.9A Ensure that commissioning products are to specification and saleable.
9.0	Contract and project close-out: To design and establish a system whereby contract compliance with the work scope and requirements can be demonstrated from both a plant completeness and operability, as well as a quality or conformance to requirements and deliverables' point of view.	A project close-out system, procedure and documentation, which can be used to successfully close-out the contract of the project, so that all monies, concessions and deviations from the work-scope and quality requirements can be settled against the 'as built' or 'as received' plant or system.	9.0 Ensure that all requirements of the scope for the deliverables actually handed over to the customer conform to specifications.

B INVESTORS and SHAREHOLDERS	C PLANT OWNERS	D LICENSORS
4.0B Reporting on quality of E D and T progress to form an integral part of the regular report to investors, including cost of non quality.	4.0C Have independent formal reviews carried out on all engineering designs. There should be a hold-point at this stage to ensure acceptability.	4.0D Have licensor designs independently reviewed for ability to meet specifications. Are specifications compatible with those of other licensors and plant suppliers or contractors of the plant concerned?
5.0B Report on quality of procured items. To form integral part of report to investors, include cost of non quality and specifications.	5.0C Plant owners to be made aware of any special quality requirements prior to the placing of the order. Reports on quality of supplied goods are necessary.	5.0D Ensure the use and achievement of common or compatible specifications with the rest of the plant equipment being purchased. Licensor to ensure that the quality of items/systems procured for his system are acceptable.
6.0B Report to investors to include quality section as well as cost of non quality. Confirm that constructed plant satisfies requirements.	6.0C Report required on quality of constructed plant on a monthly basis in terms of incidents and cost of non quality. Report to include an overview of outcome of quality assessments performed progressively.	6.0D Licensor to be responsible for the construction and quality of the relevant plant. Their quality system must be compatible with that of the project manager for the rest of the plant.
7.0B	7.0C Report required on number and complexity of errors and/or butt (punch) lists during this phase in terms of incidents and cost of non quality.	7.0D The licensor is responsible for all quality data packs which demonstrate that all relevant plant equipment and system requirements have been fully met.
8.0B Report on ease of commissioning. Report on achievement of product and waste specifications during commissioning.	8.0C Report on plant reliability. Report on achievement of product and waste specifications during commissioning. Report on cost of correcting problems identified during commissioning.	8.0D The licensor to perform commissioning tests to demonstrate that the plant supplied conforms to all the requirements. This is to be included in formal report. This is to be acceptable to the plant operators and owners.
9.0B Review planned close-out report which, amongst others, gives a review on quality of equipment and systems.	9.0C Report on non conforming plant and its influence on the rest of the plant, as well as cost of correction and cost of non quality.	9.0D Contracts can only be closed out and final payment made against formal acceptance by the operator/owner when all the requirements and specifications have been met.

	E PLANT OPERATORS	F GOVERNMENT and LOCAL AUTHORITIES	G PROJECT MANAGERS
4.0	4.0E Form a permanent part of the design and specification review team that approves designs and specifications.	4.0F Where necessary have design and technical specifications approved by the local authorities. Include inspections and reviews where necessary.	4.0G Appoint the actual project management team. The contract must make them fully responsible for quality as well. Close liaison on quality matters with owner/licensor and necessary operations personnel. All designs to be formally reviewed and accepted as per ISO 9001.
5.0	5.0E Form a permanent part of the procurement review of suppliers and proposed equipment for acceptability. Assist with the review of concessions requested by suppliers. Assist with specifying manuals needed.	5.0F Review that the requirements and specifications of services procured from local authorities are correct.	5.0G Project managers to procure or review procurement of all supplies in accordance with applicable quality management practices, i.e. ISO 9000 series. All suppliers to be quality approved.
6.0	6.0E Second operational personnel to be used on plant at the site. QA team per plant to learn the plant and its QA system during construction. Commence with preliminary operations procedures, allowing for plant construction changes.	6.0F Involve in applicable progress reporting, especially quality of construction as part of an ongoing PR process.	6.0G Ensure that all construction is carried out in accordance with designs or approved design changes. All plants to be built in accordance with quality plans, with approved data packs as evidence of conformance.
7.0	7.0E Draft commissioning procedures in conjunction with the project's managing contractor. Review plant QA documentation with site QA and QI for completeness.	7.0F	7.0G Ensure that constructed plant is as per 'build to' specification and that documented evidence exists. Identify all shortcomings in 'butt lists' and have these corrected to ensure final completeness of plant and documentation.
8.0	8.0E Form an integral part as seconded staff of the contractor's commissioning team to verify acceptability and learn hands-on plant operations.	8.0F Report on quality of product and waste, as well as action to be taken to correct problems.	8.0G Commission in accordance with operations and project management agreed procedures. Correct any shortcomings that become evident during commissioning so that plant yields product in accordance with original requirements.
9.0	9.0E Form part of the final plant acceptance team and make final settlement – also subject to operations acceptance of plant.	9.0F Review close-out report for compliance to all requirements. Close-out report to specifically address these requirements and specifications.	9.0G Project management to ensure that only projects that have been accepted by their quality management team after commissioning, are closed-out and retention monies paid out. Generate plant close-out project and report thereupon.

H ENVIRONMENT	I CONSULTANTS
4.0H Meet environmental requirements with the same diligence as the other requirements. Use ISO 14000 as basis for environmental system.	4.0I Review safety process and environmentally critical items and systems during and after design to ensure correctness and completeness.
5.0H Procure as far as possible for 'environmentally friendly' suppliers.	5.0I Audit that requirements of 7.0G are being carried out. (Carry out audit by independent group.)
6.0H Carry out construction and erection with as little disturbance/destruction of the environment as possible. Audit and report regularly that this is happening in accordance with environmental specifications.	6.0I Audit that the requirements of 8.0G and 8.0H are being carried out and that the project and quality management team is effective.
7.0H	7.0I Audit that the project management team is effective and that the precommissioning and handover documentation is complete and credible.
8.0H Ensure when any plant is started that product or waste can be treated in the correct manner.	8.0I
9.0H Review close-out report for acceptability of plant and system to the environment. This must include post-construction rehabilitated areas.	9.0I Audit that the requirements of 11.0G and 11.0H are being executed.

Quality related requirements and deliverables for a project matrix of activity sequence and involved parties

	INVOLVED PARTIES (who) ACTIVITY SEQUENCE (when)		A CUSTOMER or CLIENT
	OPERATIONAL PHASE Objectives	Deliverables	
10.0	Start up: A formal starting of the plant or system for continuous production. It is from this activity that plant and equipment guarantee periods and results in terms of availability, product quality and quantity, etc. are measured.	A plant or system operating within the design parameters that produces products or services of the desired quality and quantity.	10.0A Confirm that the products produced satisfy customer's needs in terms of both quality and quantity.
11.0	De-bottlenecking and troubleshooting: To study the plant design, capacities and layout from an operational point of view, using a benchmark plant as a reference point. This exercise must also be carried out on the operational plant to ensure optimum operating conditions.	A full report on the study, highlighting potential problem areas taking into account the following: areas of under-capacity, areas of low availability, areas where product service, specifications or quality are not achievable or maintainable, high risk areas, safety or otherwise. This report will form the basis for corrective action.	11.0A
12.0	Operation and optimization: A detailed study of the operating plant in order to optimize through-put rates, in terms of product quality and consistency, as well as system safety, reliability and availability.	A full report on the optimum operating conditions. This report is supported by the operational results, procedures and training schedules needed to establish and ensure maintenance of these conditions.	12.0A Insist system consistently gives products and waste that are acceptable to customers and stakeholders. Conduct customer surveys to establish/conform customer satisfaction with product and waste. Respond to customer's needs and requests.
13.0	Decommissioning: To establish the best decommissioning and 'mothballing' of demonstration plant or equipment.	A report and system detailing how the plant should be decommissioned optimally for: 1. 'Mothballing' 2. Demolition.	13.0A

B INVESTORS and SHAREHOLDERS	C PLANT OWNERS	D LICENSORS
10.0B Inform investors of the start up results in terms of product quality and quantity as soon as the process (and personnel) have stabilized.	10.0C The same as for investors.	10.0D 1. Keep licensor's representative on hand during this phase to ensure use of correct start up and operational procedures. 2. Establish that product quality and quantity conform to licence.
11.0B Highlight serious bottlenecks that prevent product quality and 'quantity of waste' being achieved. Quantify in monetary values what the benefits are of de-bottlenecking and improving, on a case-by-case early-care basis.	11.0C The same as for investors.	11.0D De-bottlenecking of licensed and other plant and interfaces to be performed with the licensor and final result to conform to all process requirements.
12.0B Confirm achievement of consistent product quality.	12.0C Confirm achievement of consistent product quality.	12.0D The licensed plant shall deliver product/service that conforms, as a minimum, to the original requirements.
13.0B Confirm the successful decommissioning of the plant or facility.	13.0C Report that decommissioned plant is safe and will not damage the environment. Inspect site from time to time to confirm continued compliance.	13.0D Decommission in accordance with licensor's requirements (where applicable).

	E PLANT OPERATORS	F GOVERNMENT and LOCAL AUTHORITIES	G PROJECT MANAGERS
10.0	10.0E Operate the plant in accordance with approved systems and procedures in order to: stabilize operating systems, complete learning curves for staff, demonstrate acceptability of product.	10.0F Draw up operational reports that demonstrate compliance of operational systems, procedures, product and waste, with relevant regulations.	10.0G Establish that the guarantees offered by or through the project managers are being met. A formal report to this effect must be drafted.
11.0	11.0E Take the lead in de-bottlenecking and trouble-shooting and make sure that all product and waste requirements are strictly complied with and improved upon.	11.0F	11.0G Correct the aspects of the plant or system that do not consistently comply with legal requirements.
12.0	12.0E Operate the plant in accordance with all requirements. Improve quality on a step by step, continuous basis.	12.0F Involve in continuous PR work, especially control of quality of waste, to give confidence that the environment is not being negatively influenced.	12.0G
13.0	13.0E Establish decommissioning requirements in terms of re-start up, safety and environment. Ensure that these are known and included in the original design.	13.0F Involve in decommissioning planning to demonstrate the safety and environmental friendliness of the decommissioned plant.	13.0G Establish all the decommissioning requirements and manage the contract accordingly. Audit that these have been complied with.

H ENVIRONMENT	I CONSULTANTS
10.0H After stabilization of the process draft an environmental impact report and publicize to demonstrate environmental acceptability of plant or system.	
11.0H Correct the aspects of the plant or system operation that do not constantly comply with environmental requirements.	11.0I Use operations or 'licensor' consultants only where necessary.
12.0H Operate the plant in an environmentally friendly manner. Monitor, audit and report this continually.	12.0I Use operations or 'licensor' consultants only where necessary.
13.H Plan to restore the site to its original or better condition after decommissioning.	13.0I Use operations or 'licensor' consultants only where necessary.

References

Agnihorthri, S. et al (1994) 'Managing design for quality – developing and implementing a cross-functional course', paper at Design Management Institute's 6th International Forum (Paris)

Boaden, R. J. and Dale, B. G. (1994) *Quality Management Journal*

BS 6143 Part 2 (1990) 'Guide to the economics of quality – prevention appraisal and failure model', British Standards Institute, London

BS 7000 (1989), 'Guide to managing product design', British Standards Institute, London

Burns, T. and Stalker, G. M. (1966) *Management of Innovation*, London: Tavistock

Carruthers, M. C. (1989) 'The management of quality on the Mossgas project', lecture given to the South African Society for Quality

Carruthers, M. C. (1992) 'The importance of an holistic approach during the development phase of the Soekor (oil exploration) Bredasdorp Basen project', paper given at ESKOM Project Management Conference

Crosby, P. B. (1979) *Quality is Free – The Art of Making Quality Certain*, McGraw-Hill Inc.

Dale, B. G. et al (1994) *Managing Quality*, 2nd ed., Prentice Hall

Deming, W. E. (1982) *Quality, productivity and competitive position*, Massachusetts Institute of Technology, Centre for Advanced Engineering Study, Cambridge, Massachusetts

Disney and Bendell, (1994) (contribs) *Managing Quality*, 2nd ed., Prentice Hall

Feigenbaum, A. V. (1956) 'Total quality control', *Harvard Business Review*, 34(6) 93–101

Fluor, R. J. (1977) 'Development of project managers', keynote address to the Project Management Institute, Chicago

Haynes, M. E. (1990) *Project Management from Idea to Implementation*, Kogan Page

Hutchins, D. (1992) *Achieve Total Quality*, Director Books

ISO 8402 (1994) 'Quality management and quality assurance. Vocabulary', International Organization for Standardization

ISO 9001 (1994) Quality Systems Part 1, 'Model for quality assurance in design/development, production, installation and servicing', International Organization for Standardization

ISO 9004 Part 6, 'Draft guide to quality management in project management', International Organization for Standardization

ISO/CD 10006 (1995) 'Guideline to quality in project management', International Organization for Standardization

Juran, J. and Gryna, F. M. (1980) *Quality Planning and Analysis*, McGraw-Hill

Juran, J. M. and Gryna, F. M. (1988) *Juran's Quality Control Handbook*, 4th ed., McGraw-Hill Inc.

Juran, J. M. et al (1979) *Quality Control Handbook*, McGraw-Hill Book Company

Kanter, R. M., Stein, B. A. and Jick, T. D. (1992) *The Challenge of Organizational Change*, New York, Free Press

Kerzner, H. (1989) *Project Management: A Systems Approach to Planning, Scheduling and Controlling*, Van Nostrand Reinhold Company

Kimmons, R. L. (1990) *Project Management Basics: A Step by Step Approach*, Marcel Dekker Inc.

Kimmons, R. L. and Lowrence, J. H. (eds) (1989) *Project Management: A Reference for Professionals*, Marcel Dekker Inc.

Lammermeyr, H. U. (1990) *Human Relations – the Key to Quality*, Quality Press, American Society for Quality Control and Quality Resources (a division of Kraus Organization Ltd)

Mechanical Engineering, Vol. 117, Number 2, page 80 (1995) The American Society for Mechanical Engineers (ASME), New York

Moore, F. G. (ed) (1964) *A Management Source Book*, Harper & Row, New York

Oakland, J. S. (1989) *Total Quality Management*, Butterworth Heinemann

Oakley, M. et al (1990) *Design Management*, Blackwell

Oberlender, G. D. (1993) *Project Management for Engineering and Construction*, McGraw-Hill Inc.

Oxford English Dictionary (1992) Oxford University Press

Rubach, L. (1995) 'Downsizing: How Quality is Affected as Companies Shrink', *Quality Progress*, April, p. 23

Topalian, A. (1994) 'Getting to grips with the "design dimension" of quality improvement programmes', paper at Design Management Institute's 6th International Forum (Paris)

Wiig, K. M. (1987) 'Planning for uncertainty in large projects', in *New Dimensions of Project Management* (ed. Kelley, A. J.) Lexington Books, O. C. Heath & Co, Lexington, Massachusetts

Williams, G. V. (1995) 'Fast track pros and cons: considerations for industrial projects', *Journal of Management in Engineering*, September/October (Volume 11 number 5)

Index

Note The index should be consulted together with the relevant chapter contents